Penguin Books

The Big Questions

Paul Davies is Professor of Natural Philosophy at the University of Adelaide. He is the author of some twenty books, including *The Mind of God*, *The Cosmic Blueprint*, *The Last Three Minutes*, *Are We Alone?*, *About Time* and *Superforce*. In 1995 he won the prestigious Templeton Prize, the world's largest award for intellectual endeavour, for his work on the deeper meaning of science. He has achieved international reputation for his ability to explain the significance of advanced scientific ideas in simple language.

Phillip Adams (AO) is an author, broadcaster, columnist, film-maker, achaeologist and atheist. His eleven feature films include *The Adventures of Barry McKenzie* and *Don's Party*, and his ten books include *Adams Versus God*. Co-founder of the Australian Skeptics, he was Senior ANZAC Fellow in 1981 and Australian Humanist of the Year in 1987. He was Chairman of the Australian Film Commission, the Australian Film Institute and foundation chairman of the Commission for the Future. Compere of the ABC's *Late Night Live*, he is a columnist for the *Australian*.

Other books by Paul Davies

The Ghost in the Atom (with J. R. Brown)
The Runaway Universe
God and the New Physics
The Forces of Nature
Superstrings: A Theory of Everything?
(with J. R. Brown)
Other Worlds
The Matter Myth (with John Gribbin)
The Last Three Minutes
The Mind of God
The Edge of Infinity
The Cosmic Blueprint
Are We Alone?
Superforce
About Time

Other books by Phillip Adams

Adams with Added Enzymes
The Unspeakable Adams
More Unspeakable Adams
The Uncensored Adams
The Inflammable Adams
Adams Versus God
Classic Columns
The Penguin Book of Australian Jokes
The Penguin Book of Jokes from Cyberspace
Harold Cazneaux: the Quiet Observer

THE BIG QUESTIONS

Paul Davies

in conversation with

Phillip Adams

PENGUIN BOOKS

Penguin Books Australia Ltd
487 Maroondah Highway, PO Box 257
Ringwood, Victoria 3134, Australia
Penguin Books Ltd
Harmondsworth, Middlesex, England
Viking Penguin, A Division of Penguin Books USA Inc.
375 Hudson Street, New York, New York 10014, USA
Penguin Books Canada Limited
10 Alcorn Avenue, Toronto, Ontario, Canada M4V 3B2
Penguin Books (N.Z.) Ltd
182–190 Wairau Road, Auckland 10, New Zealand

First published by Penguin Books Australia Ltd 1996
10 9 8 7 6 5 4 3 2 1
Copyright © Piper Films Pty Ltd 1996

All rights reserved. Without limiting the rights under copyright reserved above, no part of this publication may be reproduced, stored in or introduced into a retrieval system, or transmitted, in any form or by any means (electronic, mechanical, photocopying, recording or otherwise), without the prior written permission of both the copyright owner and the above publisher of this book.

Typeset in 11/15 Sabon by Post Typesetters
Made and printed in Australia by Australian Print Group

National Library of Australia
Cataloguing-in-Publication data:

Davies, P. C. W. (Paul Charles William), 1946– .
The big questions.

ISBN 0 14 025937 6.

1. Cosmology. 2. Physics – Philosophy. I. Adams, Phillip, 1939– .
II. Title. III. Title: Big questions (Television program).

523.1

Contents

	Foreword	vii
i	In the Beginning	1
ii	The Creative Cosmos	27
iii	The Riddle of Time	53
iv	The Ghost in the Machine	81
v	In Search of the Theory of Everything	103
vi	What Does It All Mean?	127
	List of Players	153

Foreword

I had read just about all of Professor Paul Davies' books whilst commuting on British Rail during 1988–89. We returned home to Adelaide following a year in London, at about the same time that Paul and his family came to Adelaide. So I thought I'd meet the author who had re-ignited my interests in the 'big questions' of physics and science more generally. This eventually led to an event at the Adelaide Town Hall (in collaboration with Phillip Adams and with help from the local arts community), in which the links between the arts and sciences were explored.

If you can do it on stage, you should also be able to do something on TV, and reach an even bigger audience. No one had previously managed to produce a television series with Paul, however. So I suggested to Mike Piper, an Adelaide-based producer, that he 'have a go' at putting something together. To abbreviate a long story, *The Big Questions* series was born – the challenge was to communicate the substance and excitement of the 'big questions' in an interesting way within the television medium, and do it within budget.

So *The Big Questions* became a gentle dialogue between Paul Davies and Phillip Adams on the great and fascinating questions of existence, against a magnificent and entirely appropriate Australian backdrop.

And now – the book of the series, which will help communicate to a further audience again.

What's next? *Big Questions II*, or perhaps *Bigger Questions*? Whatever, it will be another step in telling the story of the wonder of the universe and its exploration by science.

Mark Coleman
Adelaide, January 1996

i

In the Beginning

Phillip: *Since the year dot, humans have wondered about, and pondered upon, and come to strange conclusions concerning the Big Questions; amateur speculations giving way to the professional punditry of philosopher and theologian, and increasingly of the scientist. In these discussions, we shall examine the whys and wherefores of the cosmos; its beginning, your choice of endings, and where – if at all – humans fit in.*

Paul, I know this is just a large lump of Australia and that's not the Dead Sea down there, but have you ever wondered why the desert faiths turned out to be the most conducive to science?

Paul: I have indeed. I don't know what it is really. Perhaps something about the starkness of the landscape, the immediacy of nature – the clarity of the sky.

Phillip: Yes. A good view of the stars!

Paul: And the loneliness, the isolation. It gives you time to think.

Phillip: With all the great creation myths – and you must have studied a plethora of them – do any, in any way, vaguely accord with what science now tells us about the origin of the physical universe?

Paul: Only in the broadest sense. The monotheistic religions all have the notion that the universe did have a beginning at a finite time in the past, and science supports that point of view. The other feature that is important about the monotheistic religions is their claim that not everything got created at once. It wasn't a matter of 'Hey presto!' and suddenly here it all was intact. The biblical version of creation, for example, involved a definite sequence of steps before the present form of the world came to exist, and scientific cosmology makes the same claim. So to that extent the biblical creation story parallels the modern scientific picture, but I don't think one should read anything deep into that.

Phillip: People try to do that – desperately.

Paul: Well, they do, and I think it is entirely

misconceived. There is no reason to suppose that the people who wrote these ancient texts had a scientific view of the world. Inasmuch as we find parallels, they are interesting, but I don't think they prove some sort of deep revelatory knowledge about the universe.

Phillip: Odd that only the Hindus seem to have a concept of deep time.

Paul: Curiously the Hindu religion actually overdoes it, because the biggest of the Hindu cycles is much longer than the supposed age of the universe, according to modern cosmology. But you're quite right about the shallow time scale in the Bible, which on a literal interpretation is absurdly short. Personally I think that the hopelessly incorrect age of the universe here is less important than the key fact that in all three of these religions – Judaism, Islam and Christianity – the universe actually *has* an origin in time, and is not cyclic as in so many other ancient cosmologies. And not only that. The monotheistic religions not only have the universe coming into being at some particular moment, they also make use of so-called linear time – a unidirectional sequence of events with a beginning, middle, and end. There is a cosmic story to tell!

Phillip: Hence the latter-day prophets who replace a

creation myth with the big bang theory.

Paul: That's right. The mechanism of the coming-into-being of the universe, as discussed in modern science, is actually much more profound than the biblical version because it does not merely involve order emerging out of chaos. It's not just a matter of imposing some sort of organisation or structure upon a previous incoherent state, but literally the coming-into-being of all physical things from nothing.

Phillip: It's an irony, isn't it, that the term 'big bang' was originally a pejorative – a joke – by the British astronomer Fred Hoyle, who wouldn't have a bar of it.

Paul: Yes, it is ironical. That was in the 1950s, but the basis of the big bang theory goes back much farther, to 1915 and Einstein's general theory of relativity. However, it wasn't until the 1920s, when Edwin Hubble discovered that the universe was expanding, that scientists really envisaged an abrupt beginning, a primeval state in which everything was very compressed and flying out of some sort of singularity.

Phillip: But there were people who anticipated the singularity long before the observational evidence, weren't there?

Paul: Yes, curiously enough there was. In 1921 a Russian meteorologist, Alexander Friedman, took the equations from Einstein's general theory of relativity – which is really a theory of gravitation, space and time – and solved them to produce what turns out to be a pretty good fit to the observational data describing an expanding universe. A distinctive feature of Friedman's model is that it describes a universe which originates at a finite moment in the past from a singular state of infinite density – a singularity – in a gigantic explosive outburst. It then goes on expanding, but at a diminishing rate, to an uncertain fate. Friedman sent his solutions of Einstein's equations to Einstein himself, but the great man wasn't terribly impressed. He noted Friedman's work and thought it was interesting, but shrugged it aside. It was another ten years until, on a visit to the United States, Einstein met Edwin Hubble and learned that the universe is expanding. Only then did he begin to take the idea seriously.

By the mid-1930s not only Einstein, but many scientists, were taking seriously the basic idea of what we would now call the big bang theory. However, it had to wait until after the Second World War, and in particular the work of the cosmologist George Gamow, for the big bang theory to become part of mainstream science. Gamow promoted the idea that if the universe did begin in some sort of highly compressed state with an explosive outburst, it may have left an imprint in the universe today in the form of heat radiation left over from the initial explosion.

Now, Fred Hoyle was an arch opponent of the big bang theory, preferring instead his own so-called steady state theory of the universe, in which there is no abrupt beginning; the universe is hypothesised to be infinitely old. Hoyle derisively compared the conventional theory of Gamow and company to a sort of cosmic conjuring trick – a universe originating with an unexplained 'big bang'. And of course the name stuck.

A curious aside: I learned on my travels recently that there has been a sort of straw poll among astronomers in the United States to come up with a better term than the big bang theory. After all the suggestions were sent in and the scores added up, the judges found that the most popular term was in fact the big bang theory!

Phillip: While the deep waters that once covered this ancient land may have receded long ago, I'm now going to get back into them. It seems that once upon a time, we asked our priests to explain the world, and they gave us metaphor and myth. Yet their explanations had the virtue – the great virtue – of being comprehensible. The trouble with your stuff, Paul, is that it is immensely difficult for the ordinary punter to accommodate in the neurons! You're going to tell me, as I understand it, that the big bang occurs out of nothing, in a context where there is no time and no space. Now, you can tell me that until the cows come home, until they're fossilised, and I will still find it impossible to understand.

Paul: It's undeniably true that many of the concepts of modern physics and cosmology are counter-intuitive; they seem to defy common sense. In particular they are very hard to visualise. People often get worried about that. They think that if they can't imagine something in their mind's eye, then somehow they don't understand it, or that it must be wrong. I don't think that is true. The power of science is precisely that it can take us into territories where common sense and intuition fail us, and yet still lead us in the direction of reliable knowledge.

Phillip: Well, we've got time to come back to this, but for now let's dwell on this extraordinary instant where time begins.

Paul: Yes. So this big bang thing is more than just the explosion of a lump of something in a pre-existing void. A lot of people have that misconception. They imagine something like huge empty space with a sort of cosmic egg sitting in the middle of it for all eternity – just sitting there and sitting there. Then suddenly – BANG! – the whole thing flies apart, and the fragments, our galaxy being one of them, all go shooting off. Well, it's wrong, wrong, wrong! That is *not* the way to think of the universe.

We know that the universe is expanding; we know the galaxies are retreating from us and from each other. The whole system is getting bigger and bigger with time. How can one envisage that? Well, don't make the mistake of imagining that the galaxies are all rushing away from a common centre, because they're not. What is actually happening is that the *space between* the galaxies is swelling or stretching –

Phillip: A bit like points on a balloon's skin?

Paul: Correct. Imagine little dots on the surface of a balloon: if you were to inflate the balloon, each dot would move away from every other dot. Now, when you use that analogy people immediately jump to the wrong conclusion that somehow the universe corresponds to the volume *within* the balloon. It doesn't. I'm using the analogy of a two-dimensional elastic surface (the fabric of the balloon) to represent the three dimensions of space in the real universe.

Phillip: Incidentally, how do we know the universe is expanding like this? What led Hubble to make that claim?

Paul: Hubble arrived at this monumental conclusion in the late 1920s when he noticed that the galaxies that are further away from us have somewhat redder light; this is the famous 'red shift'. He interpreted this in terms of the stretching or elongation of the light waves caused by motion, known as the Doppler effect. A shift towards the red, or long wavelength, end of the light spectrum tells us that the object is receding.

We now have an equivalent but more appealing way to think of the cosmological red shift. As light travels across the universe, through space that is itself swelling or stretching, then the light waves also get stretched. As a result, these light waves arrive on Earth with wavelengths a bit longer than they had when they were emitted by the distant galaxy. So that is how we know that the universe is expanding.

Coming back to the idea of the origin of time, the best way I can try to explain it is to invite you to imagine the expanding balloon that represents space, viewed in reversed time. As you go back in time the balloon is smaller and smaller. Imagine it shrinking down, and down, and down, until it's just a little dot – a single point of space. All of the fabric of the balloon is concentrated into that single point, like the apex of a cone. And that point, that apex, is the end – or in this case, the beginning. Beyond the point is nothing. The balloon – space – has simply disappeared. Play this scenario in forward time and it represents the coming-into-being of a universe from literally nothing, with space itself appearing. So it's not an explosion in a pre-existing space. Space *itself* appears. And so, for that matter, does time. Einstein taught us that space and time are intimately interwoven. Where one goes the other goes. There can be no time without space. If space comes into existence abruptly at the big bang, then time comes into existence abruptly, too.

What does this mean? It means that there was *no time before the big bang*. This is an absolutely fundamental point. People often ask what happened before the big bang, or what caused the big bang –

Phillip: Paul, you can't blame them, can you?

Paul: No, no! It's a very natural question.

Phillip: Given the way we're wired.

Paul: It's a very natural question – cause and effect. You probe back in time, tracing the cause of each cosmic event in some earlier event. You push it further and further back until you reach the point we call the big bang, and naturally enough you want to ask, 'Well, what made the big bang go bang? What caused it? What was there before it?' And the scientific answer is – nothing! And by 'nothing' I don't mean empty space. I mean, no matter, no energy, no space and no time. In other words 'no *thing*' in the normal sense of the word 'thing'. In particular, there simply was no *before* for anything to happen *in*, because time itself began with the big bang.

Phillip: I know we're going to try and quarantine discussions about God to the end. Nonetheless, Paul, it seems appropriate to introduce your old pal Augustine – your favourite theologian – here. Didn't he have a glimmering of the notion of time beginning in this way?

Paul: Absolutely. Augustine had two brilliant insights into the nature of time. One of them is that we all know what time is until somebody asks us, and then we're lost for words. That is very good, I think! The other is the idea that the universe itself came into being with time. The way Augustine expressed it was that 'the world was made *with* time and not *in* time'. He recognised that time itself is part of the physical universe. And so if the physical universe was going to be created by God then God had better create time, too.

I might say that Augustine arrived at this conclusion on theological rather than physical grounds. He was partly responding to the old problem concerning what God was doing before she created the universe. The standard answer was, 'Busy creating hell for the likes of you!' So Augustine came up with this notion that time itself must have begun with the physical world; there was no infinite duration in which God deliberated but desisted from creating the universe. However, it wasn't until Einstein's theory of relativity that the concept of time being part of the physical universe, and therefore originating with the physical universe, was placed on a firm scientific footing. So although the idea is admittedly very hard to wrap your imagination around, it's actually 1500 years old. Augustine was already there in the fifth century with the concept.

Phillip: Let me ask you for more proof of the truth of the big bang, more solid evidence.

Paul: If the theory were based on the expansion of the universe alone, I think we would be right to be sceptical. But there are other strands of evidence as well, really rather powerful. Perhaps the most important of these was the discovery, in the 1960s, that the entire universe is bathed in heat radiation. It's rather like us all living in a gigantic microwave oven. Wherever you look in the sky there is heat radiation – microwaves – with a temperature of about three degrees above absolute zero. That's not very hot; it's not going to do you any harm, but it is very noticeable. Now, it's almost impossible to explain where this radiation has come from, other than supposing it originated in the big bang. It's *primeval* heat, left over from the birth of the cosmos, just as Gamow predicted.

Phillip: Some sort of detritus from the detonation?

Paul: Well, I would say afterglow.

The significance of this radiation is that it gives us a clue about the state of the universe shortly after the beginning. I was a student in the mid-sixties, and I can well remember the professor in my department giving a lecture about cosmology, talking about the origin of the universe, and saying that on the basis of the recent discovery of the cosmic heat radiation it was possible to reconstruct the physics of events that took place in the first *three minutes* after the big bang! And everyone fell about laughing. They thought it was utterly audacious to hypothesise about what happened just a few minutes after the origin of the universe. Yet today this is standard textbook stuff.

Phillip: Not only textbook stuff, but demonstrable, reproducible in laboratories.

Paul: That's right. This is, I think, a very important point that a lot of people don't realise. Because we're dealing here with huge numbers and extreme conditions, it all seems way beyond human experience, and impossible to test. But that's not true. For example, from measurements of the cosmic heat radiation it is simple to work out that one second after the big bang the temperature of the universe was about ten billion degrees. Now that sounds like an awfully high temperature, but it is well within the capability of our laboratories to reproduce.

Phillip: How?

Paul: Using particle accelerator machines – huge ring-shape machines –

Phillip: That governments will no longer pay for –

Paul: That governments will no longer pay for. At least not the biggest we would like.

These machines accelerate particles like electrons and protons round and round inside ring-shaped tubes, and then smash them together. And they can do this with such force that the energies involved correspond to temperatures of trillions of degrees. In that way one can directly recreate – albeit fleetingly – the conditions that would have prevailed, not just one second after the big bang, nor even a microsecond, but a *trillionth* of a second!

Using particle-collisions experiments and other techniques, we can go some way to modelling the nuclear and particle physics processes that would have occurred in the early moments of the universe, and determine whether there might be some trace or relic left in the universe today that may confirm the theory. And remarkably enough there is at least one such relic: the element helium. Helium was first discovered in the sun, but is now a familiar element in the universe. Although it is rather rare on earth, it turns out that about 25 per cent of the universe as a whole is made of helium. Pretty well all the rest is made of hydrogen. The stuff that you and I are made of – you know, carbon, oxygen and nitrogen, and so on – are really just tiny impurities in a universe overwhelmingly made of hydrogen and helium. So, on a cosmic scale, the relative abundances of the elements are roughly three-quarters hydrogen and one-quarter helium. Now, this numerical ratio of hydrogen to helium is very nicely explained by computing the nuclear processes that occurred in the primeval furnace during the first three minutes.

Phillip: Well, what about the rest of the role call, what about the remaining inventory of elements?

Paul: Oh, this is a fascinating one! Because the stuff of our bodies – the carbon and the oxygen and so on – wasn't there at the beginning. It wasn't coughed out of the big bang, so to speak. These heavier elements were manufactured inside stars. Large stars manufacture chemical elements by nuclear processes in their cores. Now, large stars don't live very long; they burn fuel furiously and end their days spectacularly by blowing themselves to bits in explosions called supernovae. When this happens to a star it spews its material into space, heavy elements and all. When the next generation of stars, and maybe planets, forms, some of these heavier elements – spread among the ashes of dead stars – get scooped up. So in a very real sense, you and I are made of stardust.

Phillip: May this pile of impurities ask you this? Is it game, set and match for the big bang theory? Aren't there a lot of rather large details to be hammered out? Anomalies to be dealt with? For example, isn't there a major dispute about the age of the universe?

Paul: Yes. It would be very surprising if a simple model like this explained everything in one go, just like that! I think the *fact* of the big bang – that the universe began abruptly at some finite moment in the past – is thoroughly established. There are very few scientists, very few cosmologists, who would dispute that. But there are lively arguments over the precise details, and in particular you mentioned one: the age of the universe. This is a very old problem. In fact, it goes right back to the time of Hubble's early measurements.

Hubble, you will recall, measured the *rate* at which the universe is expanding; how fast it's getting bigger and bigger. By playing the great cosmic movie backwards you can get some idea of how long ago everything was all together, corresponding to when the big bang occurred. Now, of course if the universe expanded at the same rate for all time, that would be a trivial calculation to do. If you take Hubble's figures, and make the assumption of a constant expansion rate, you come up with an age of about two billion years. Well, that is clearly not right, because we know the Earth is 4.5 billion years old. That is the age of the material of the Earth as determined from radioactive decay. Clearly the universe has got to be at least that age. And from careful measurements of ancient stars in globular clusters, astronomers believe that the oldest stars have been around for at least fourteen or fifteen billion years.

Since Hubble's day, astronomers have revised their estimates of the age of the universe upwards and upwards. For a long while there was a sort of uneasy truce, in which it was accepted that with a little bit of fudging and fitting you could just about accommodate the oldest stars in a universe with a rather suspiciously short age. However, this tight fit has come apart at the seams recently. The Hubble space telescope is able to provide a much more accurate measurement of the rate at which the universe is expanding, and again, if you take a simple model you can convert that rate into an age of the universe. The figure comes out to be about eight, nine, or ten billion years – far too short to accommodate those ancient stars.

Now, it's not all hopeless for the big bang theory, I might say, because the rate of expansion surely has *not* remained constant with time.

The universe began explosively, with everything rushing apart very fast, but as time went on the rate of expansion diminished – for a very simple reason. In cosmology the only force in town is gravitation. Gravitation is a pulling force, as you can see by simply dropping a stone; it's pulled towards the earth. Well, the sun pulls on the Earth, the stars pull on each other, the galaxies attract each other, and so on. Everything in the universe attracts everything else –

Phillip: And that puts the foot on the brake, in effect.

Paul: Exactly. We have this explosive beginning with the universe initially expanding very rapidly, but gravity trying to drag it back, so that the universe slows in its rate of expansion, like a braking effect. So if you measure the rate of expansion of the universe today, which is what astronomers have done with the Hubble space telescope, for example, you can't immediately convert that figure into an estimate of the age of the universe unless you also know the strength of this braking effect. And the degree of braking depends in turn on the amount of matter that there is in the universe. The more material the universe contains, the greater the total gravitational pull, and the faster the universe decelerates. But there is a big mystery about exactly how much matter there is.

Phillip: And you've got dark matter coming into that equation.

Paul: That's the point. If what you see is what you get – if the visible matter such as stars accounts for all the matter there is – then you come up with a certain age. But if in addition to the luminous matter there is a lot of unseen stuff – dark or inconspicuous material of one sort or another – then there would be more braking, and you come up with a shorter age.

The trouble is, we don't know how much dark matter is out there. We know there is a certain amount. There is very good evidence, for example, in the way the stars orbit around our Milky Way galaxy, that there's quite a lot of unseen matter accelerating them. The galaxy is revolving much too fast for the stars to be trapped in orbit by the visible matter alone. If the only material in the galaxy were the glowing, shining stuff – like stars and the gas – then the galaxy would be flung apart like an exploding flywheel. So there is obviously a lot of dark or invisible matter tugging on the stars out on the periphery of the galaxy, holding them in orbit. And by similar reasoning there is clearly a lot of matter between the galaxies.

Recently there have been attempts to identify some of this dark matter. We may envisage the familiar disk-shaped Milky Way to be imbedded in a sort of gigantic spherical halo of dark matter. Observations performed at Mount Stromlo Observatory here in Australia, and elsewhere, suggest that some of this dark matter is in the form of very dim stars located in the halo of the Milky Way. But almost certainly dim stars do not constitute all the dark matter that there is.

So you see, the uncertainty in the quantity of dark matter translates into an uncertainty about the age of the universe. The less dark matter there is, the older the universe can be for a given rate of expansion today. But even assuming that there is little or no dark matter, the age of the universe according to conventional theory is still uncomfortably short – short enough that some cosmologists are proposing a radical rethink. Personally I believe that it may be necessary to modify Einstein's general theory of relativity a bit, in a way that Einstein himself suggested in 1917. But that is a topic for another discussion.

Phillip: Paul, if there's some dispute about the date of the cosmic birth date, is there also disputation about the use-by date, about the end of time?

Paul: Yes, very much so. According to the orthodox theory, there are two very different possibilities for the cosmic demise. One is that the universe will go on expanding for ever and ever, at a diminishing rate. The other is that it will reach a state of maximum distension, after which the whole universe will start to contract, with the galaxies moving back together again. The shrinkage will begin slowly and then gather pace – faster and faster – until the entire cosmos obliterates itself at a 'big crunch', which is a bit like the big bang in reverse. So we have these two possibilities. Which of the two will come about depends on exactly how much dark matter there is in the universe. If there is a lot, then the universe will eventually collapse.

Phillip: There was, briefly, a fashionable idea that I was very much attracted to. This envisaged an oscillating universe – an infinite succession and regression of big bangs.

Paul: Bangs and crunches and bangs and crunches, yes: the so-called oscillating or pulsating model of the universe. That theory has never appealed to me very much because it seems to me that it doesn't really solve any problems. If the universe has been cycling along like that for ever and ever then clearly it has always existed in one form or another. But of course you don't explain something by supposing it's always been there. So the existence of a universe just has to be accepted as given; there is no explanation for its coming-into-being.

There is, however, a more serious problem, of a physical nature. There are many physical processes occurring in the universe that proceed at a finite rate, and are *irreversible*. For example, the formation and death of stars, and the emission of starlight into space. You can't run these processes backwards. But if the universe is infinitely old, then these irreversible processes would have all run their course by now, and the entire universe would have reached its final state. But that hasn't happened yet, so the universe can't have existed for ever. We know there must have been an absolute beginning a finite time ago.

Sometimes people try to circumvent the problem of irreversible processes by conjecturing that the universe does indeed oscillate for ever, but that each individual cycle is somehow disconnected from the previous cycle. In other words, supposing when the universe went crunch, and bounced into a new big bang, that matter and energy were totally reprocessed in such a way that no memory of the previous phase could survive.

Phillip: Yes! A great idea. That is why I found it so satisfying –

Paul: Maybe. But there is then a problem about calling this an oscillating universe. If nothing from this cycle of the universe survives into the next, there's no particular reason to regard the next cycle of expansion and contraction as 'this' universe doing something in the future. If literally no information about our cycle can get through, what meaning is there in the claim that we are dealing with a sequential thing – that is, the *same* universe undergoing a sequence of cycles? You might just as well say that the other cycles of expansion and contraction are occurring 'in parallel' to ours.

The situation is reminiscent of a variant of reincarnation, in which no memory of one's previous life ever survives. In that case, what would it mean for someone to say that *you* are the reincarnation of Napoleon rather than *I*? Neither can remember, so neither has any connection with Napoleon. Reincarnation without memory – or some quality surviving – is simply a meaningless concept.

So I think that this idea of an oscillating universe, whilst it has a certain appeal and is vaguely reminiscent of those Hindu cosmic cycles, doesn't make a lot of sense either philosophically or physically. I'm afraid we have to accept that the only two alternatives on offer are either that the universe is going to go on expanding for ever and ever, or it is going to reach a state of maximum expansion and then collapse to a big crunch.

It's one or the other.

ii

The Creative Cosmos

Phillip: *Nature: a continual struggle between order and chaos. It was from this struggle that the complexity of the world about us emerged, from snowflakes to star clusters, from bacteria to brains. Nothing less than the fate of the universe hinges on the final outcome. Although scientists are only beginning to understand how complex order arises, a fundamental law of cosmic disorder has been known for a long time.*

Paul, among the laws that govern the universe, there are three rather melancholy municipal regulations. Firstly, Murphy's Law. Secondly, Catch-22. And then there's the really bad one.

Paul: Yes. The grand-daddy of them all has got to be the second law of thermodynamics.

Phillip: Incidentally, what's the first law? We never hear about that.

Paul: Oh, yes you do. It's really the law of conservation of energy, and it just says that heat is a form of energy. Thermodynamics is the subject that investigates the exchange of heat and energy. So it was very big in the nineteenth century with the invention of heat engines and steam engines and so on.

Phillip: But the second law is really the death notice for the universe, isn't it?

Paul: That's right. But it didn't start out that way. It began innocuously enough with the investigation of the efficiency of engines. The industrialists in the nineteenth century wanted to discover if there was any limit in principle to the efficiency of heat engines and steam engines. If you were ever so clever, could you have 100 per cent conversion of heat into work, for example? Well, it turns out that for very fundamental reasons you can't achieve this. There are basic limitations imposed by the laws of nature on the efficiency of heat engines.

So far so good. But then these laws of thermodynamics were applied to the universe as a whole, quite outside the domain of human machines. In particular, the second law of thermodynamics was found to have universal applicability, and it led to a shocking prediction. It was stated in its most gloomy form by the German physicist Herman von Helmholtz in the 1850s. He pronounced that the entire universe is dying, choking so to speak, on its own entropy.

Let me explain the concept of entropy. One of the ways of thinking about the second law of thermodynamics is that all physical systems, however efficient they are, inevitably undergo some sort of degeneration over time. The ordered energy within them degrades into disordered energy or chaos. Physicists measure the degree of chaos using a precise mathematical quantity called entropy. So you can think of the amount of entropy in a system as roughly the degree of disorder it possesses. The second law of thermodynamics, when applied to the universe as a whole, states that in any physical process the entropy of the entire universe goes up a little bit; the universe overall gets a little bit more chaotic.

Phillip: Well, in practical terms this law means we not only have to deal with personal mortality but with the mortality of the whole shebang. Now, one of the first people to react, quite spectacularly, against the second law of thermodynamics, was the British philosopher Bertrand Russell. While Russell didn't argue about the truth of the second law, he was most upset by its implications. Why was that?

Paul: The reason that Russell was profoundly affected by the second law of thermodynamics was because he figured that if the entire universe is doomed, then ultimately, all humanity's striving counts for nothing. There is a famous quote in which he talks about all our hopes and fears and aspirations, all our striving – 'all the noonday brightness of human genius' were the words he used – being lost in 'the vast death of the solar system'. I think there are a lot of people who would agree that human life is ultimately futile if the entire universe itself is doomed.

Phillip: Well, count me amongst their number, Paul, because it has always seemed to me that this law, which one cannot break, in fact informs the pessimism of our century. To a large extent it may account for the anti-science feeling in contemporary society, to the widespread reaction against science, and the popularity of the existential movement.

Paul: I agree. Throughout history there have been various paradigms or models for the universe as a whole. In ancient Greece the Pythagoreans thought that the entire cosmos was a manifestation of music and number and geometry –

Phillip: The harmony of the spheres.

Paul: That's right. Then Aristotle perceived the cosmos as a gigantic organism, a living thing. Centuries later, Newton proposed that the universe is like a huge clockwork mechanism, slavishly moving towards some destiny that has been programmed into it since time immemorial. The prevailing nineteenth-century image of the universe was, by analogy with a heat engine, a thermodynamic universe dying, degenerating, running out of fuel, running out of steam. Curiously, in recent years attempts have been made to argue that the universe as a whole is like a gigantic computer, and that nature is a computational process. So each age brings with it an image of the universe, a world view, which reflects the prevailing technology of the time. Each view is incomplete, of course, but each captures, in one form or another, some important aspect of cosmic change.

Phillip: When we were children, I suspect we both had the experience of being sat on a board in a barber's chair to have our hair cut. Though I could barely read, I vividly recall being perched up there looking at a magazine which proclaimed that the sun was going to go out in a billion years. At the age of five, that was an appalling prospect. For us to contemplate the end of literally everything is beyond belief, beyond bearing.

Paul: The conclusion that the sun will one day burn out is the obvious and most conspicuous application of this second law of thermodynamics. When you stop to think about it, it *is* inevitable, because the sun can't keep burning for ever and ever. Quite simply, it's going to run out of fuel.

Now, the sun is but one of a myriad stars. Furthermore, as old stars die, so new stars are born. However, the same inexorable processes that ensure that the sun will eventually cool and fade govern the life cycles of all stars; they will all die – burn out – eventually. And because the stock of raw material to create new stars is finite, in the fullness of time no new stars will arise to replace the dying ones. So you reach the inescapable conclusion that the whole universe is slowly sliding towards a final state of degeneration (often called the heat death) in which the stars are all burned out, and the heat and light is scattered chaotically through the depths of space. It *is* a depressing prospect.

Phillip: The good news is your conviction that there's another great force to counter the second law.

Paul: I don't like the word 'force' because it implies there's some sort of supernatural manipulation going alongside the conventional forces of nature that we recognise. It's not a question of a force, as such, it's more a question of a natural tendency. Let me just try and explain this. For a hundred years, scientists and philosophers have dwelled excessively on the gloomy aspects of cosmic degeneration we've just been talking about, the fact that the entire universe is on a sort of one-way slide towards a final heat death.

Now let me raise the question: Is this image of a dying universe the most appropriate characterisation of cosmic change? If you ask about the history of the universe so far – that is, what has happened since the beginning – if you ask, 'Has it been a story of degeneration and decline?' the answer is clearly no. From what we understand about the earliest moments after the big bang, the universe was in a more or less featureless state – no more than a uniform soup of subatomic particles, and perhaps just expanding empty space. All the richness and diversity and variety of physical forms and systems we see around us today – the galaxies and stars, the clouds, the trees, the people, and so on – weren't there at the beginning. They emerged slowly in a long and complicated sequence of self-organising and self-complexifying processes.

I might say that there is nothing miraculous

about this emergence of complex organisation. The laws of nature are such that they encourage matter and energy to develop in the direction of ever-greater complexity, ever-greater richness.

Phillip: But at least this epic form of evolution – from hot soup of subatomic particles to stars and trees and people – is very positive.

Paul: That's the whole point. When you look back over the history of the universe, you don't see a story of Paradise Lost. You don't see a record of degeneration from primordial complexity; you see a history of what I might call progress – an advance from simple beginnings to complex outcomes, of featureless origins to richness and diversity.

Phillip: You realise that it is politically incorrect to talk about progress, don't you?

Paul: That's absolutely right, because progress implies some sort of value judgement, that in some sense the present state of the universe, including the existence of human beings, is somehow better than the universe was, say, five or six billion years ago. Well, we can come back to that topic, but the important point to make here is that there is undeniably a trend from simple to complex, from uniformity to variety, from featurelessness to richness. It's like a law of nature. It's clearly not an infallible law, however, because if the Earth were zapped tomorrow by a huge asteroid, it would obviously set back the complexity, at least of this planet, by a considerable amount. But nevertheless, taken overall, the story of the universe so far is the story of – I'm going to use it again – progress – the advance of complexity and organisation.

Now you might think that there's a conflict here –

Phillip: At least a paradox with a capital P.

Paul: Indeed. People have often regarded the emergence of complex order out of primordial chaos as paradoxical. They point out that the second law of thermodynamics insists that things are degenerating and dying. And yet we see many examples of the opposite. The most conspicuous of these examples is biological evolution. Generally speaking, over evolutionary history things seem to have got better and better rather than worse and worse. So there seems to be a contradiction.

In fact there is no incompatibility here. It's very important to realise that any advance of complexity, wherever it occurs in the universe, comes at a price – an entropic price. Every time a new, more highly organised, physical form or system comes into existence, the total entropy of the universe goes up a bit. Again, the most obvious example is in biology. When a baby is born and grows up to adulthood, resources – food, material, useful energy – are expended. When a new species emerges there is also a price to be paid in extra entropy in the environment, because for each successful mutant there are scores of unsuccessful ones that die –

Phillip: Paul, basically, you're not changing the pessimistic outcome, are you? There's a battle to the death between organisation and entropy. Entropy will win, but until it does we're going to –

Paul: Well, we don't know that entropy is going to win. All we can say is that we've got two arrows of time, as I prefer to call them: the pessimistic arrow which focuses upon the degeneration, and the optimistic arrow, which dwells on the emergence of complexity and organisation. They're both present, and although the one is not strictly the opposite of the other – it's not actually a zero-sum game – nevertheless it's quite clear that at the end of the day the one or the other is going to win. And people always want to know which. In the very, very far future of the universe, will the second law of thermodynamics triumph, as Bertrand Russell supposed? Will the universe simply run out of sources of useful energy – energy needed to keep this marvellous complexification and self-organisation going? Well, the answer is: we don't know. It depends on the fine details. From the most careful projections of the present state of the universe into the immensely distant future, one cannot actually be sure, given our limited understanding, whether the universe will in fact completely die.

Phillip: One of the things that has to be said about nature is its immense fecundity, not simply the way its life forms proliferate, but the *waste* in its experiments.

Paul: Yes. It's quite an extraordinary thing. I once took the trouble to calculate what, in monetary terms at today's prices, the sun is spending every second, pouring all that heat and light out into space. It turns out to be about a hundred billion billion dollars! And out of all the energy that pours forth from the sun, only two-billionths strikes the surface of the earth, and only a tiny fraction of that does any good, so to speak. The rest is just wasted, most of it going off into the depths of space never to return.

Phillip: Well, we're not in the most, shall we say, lush of environments here in the South Australian desert, but the fossil record constantly reminds us that for every living critter there seem to be thousands of experiments with life which failed or were forgotten.

Paul: Yes. As I mentioned a moment ago, the emergence of new biological species provides a very good example of the second law of thermodynamics at work. The survivors of the great game of Darwinian evolution are the successful mutations. But the fossil record is littered with examples of less successful species, or of those that couldn't adapt to changing circumstances in time, and died out. That is the entropic price paid for the success of the survivors. So nature works on the basis of this enormous profligacy – pouring out energy into space, creating enormous numbers of species, the vast majority of which don't survive for very long. Yet the end product is something which is in some sense good. In some sense there is progress. Who could deny that the state of the universe today represents an advance on what it was like one second after the big bang?

Phillip: But this arrow of progress isn't very well targeted. It's flying in a rather random fashion?

Paul: The French biologist Jacques Monod liked to use the terms 'chance' and 'necessity' in connection with biology, but we can apply it to nature as a whole. We observe that nature is ordered in a law-like manner; we are not presented with cosmic anarchy. This order we express in terms of laws, such as the laws of physics, which in some sense compel matter and energy to do certain things, they make it necessary. For example, when we say that a stone falls to the ground because of the *law* of gravity, we imply that the stone *necessarily* falls. Hence *necessity* – it is necessarily so. However, there exists alongside this necessity what we might call probabilistic events, chance events, things which are not seemingly legislated for. They just happen. Like the fall of a dice.

Now, both chance and necessity are built into physics in a very, very fundamental way. Even at the atomic level there is chance, indeterminism. But there is also necessity in the form of atomic laws. It seems to me that the universe is an exquisite mix of chance and necessity. If it were much more chancy then everything would degenerate into cosmic chaos; there would be no discernible order in nature. If there were more necessity, this would likely lead to a sort of regimented uniformity, where nothing very much of interest would happen. Instead, many physical forms and systems live on what we may call the edge of chaos. That is to say, there's enough randomness and unpredictability there to leave their future direction open. In some sense they have a freedom to explore many alternative pathways, yet they are sufficiently law-like in their behaviour to maintain some coherence and identity.

Phillip: But edges are invariably interesting, aren't they? The most interesting things in the arts, in society, in science, seem to happen at the edges.

Paul: Yes, because that's where the complicated phenomena occur. It seems to me that the emergence of organised complexity in the universe – including the emergence of life and consciousness, and maybe even technology – as a general trend, is written into the laws of nature in a very basic way. But the specific details are not, they're left to chance. So if, to take the example again, this great asteroid comes in and zaps the Earth and destroys all life except the most primitive organisms, and the great biological drama is allowed to have a second run, what will happen next time? Suppose you could come back in four billion years? Would you find *homo sapiens* here again? Would humans re-emerge? Well, the answer is clearly no. There are so many aspects of the human body and the human mind that depend on little accidents, little quirks along the evolutionary way, that it's inconceivable you would get get anything like *homo sapiens* a second time around.

Now, most biologists would say that you would not even get consciousness and intelligence emerging next time around. They insist that evolution is blind, that at the bottom of it all it is just the random shuffling of genes. If so, the population of organisms is just doing a sort of random walk through the space of possibilities, and there can be no directionality, no evolutionary trends.

I have to say that I believe this orthodox view is misconceived. I come at it from the point of view of a physicist. The inanimate world contains many examples of matter and energy being encouraged, so to speak, to develop along certain paths of evolution that lead to greater organisation and complexity. We see such a trend in the way that the primeval soup of particles just after the big bang was transformed into the complexity of the galaxy we now live in. We see it in the way that simple fluids can become turbulent and produce coherent shapes and elaborate patterns. Think of the rings of Saturn or the filigree patterns in the surface of Jupiter. These examples do not involve Darwinian natural selection. They do not involve mutating genes; there are no genes for a snowflake or a convection cell or the great red spot of Jupiter. Such patterns arise spontaneously. So we see self-organisation going on all around us in nature – the emergence of complexity and organisation – entirely spontaneously and naturally. There's nothing supernatural here, no guiding hand.

Now, I take the point of view that if organisation and complexity spontaneously emerges and advances in a highly non-random, trend-like manner in astronomy, chemistry, physics and geology, why cannot the same be true of biology?

Phillip: Let's transpose those self-organising processes to a hypothetical planet somewhere. The right amount of time passes, gradually the complexities become more complex. You are now suggesting that the laws of nature will inevitably tend to give rise to consciousness, to intelligence? Even to a species who would be mathematically sophisticated? Yet there would remain many differences. They might have no sensitivity to many of the things that intrigue or delight us. They may not respond, for example, to our art or our music.

Paul: Let me answer that by first considering the origin of life. There are three hypotheses. One is that it is a miracle. Well, I'm a scientist, I don't believe in miracles, so I'm going to reject that one. It doesn't explain life at all. The second hypothesis is that the origin of life was a stupendously improbable accident, a freak, something that almost certainly wouldn't happen a second time somewhere else in the universe. And the third hypothesis is that life is a natural by-product, a natural part of the outworkings, of the laws of physics. That is my belief: that the emergence of life, and indeed consciousness, is part of this natural outworking of physical law, this trend from simple to complex that I've been talking about. Therefore, if it occurred on earth we would expect it to occur elsewhere in the universe, too.

A test of my ideas is to search for life elsewhere in the universe. Now, that may be a hopeless search because the universe is very big. The distances between the stars are just vast, and it seems improbable that in the foreseeable future we are ever going to be able to travel to other star systems. We might just possibly get to other planets in our solar system, but they are not very promising from the point of view of life.

Fortunately there is another possibility, although it remains a long shot. If it's the case that life has evolved, as I am claiming, along a general trend towards the emergence of intelligence and technology, then we might expect there to exist advanced alien beings out there in the galaxy – beings who may have achieved intelligence and technology a long time before *homo sapiens*. If so, it's just possible that they will be trying to contact us using, for example, radio signals or laser signals. There is a long and somewhat tortured history of astronomers using radio telescopes – including here in Australia – to listen in to see if there are any messages from aliens coming our way –

Phillip: And there's also been the 'message in the bottle' that Carl Sagan and his colleagues stuck in one of our rockets – in the hope that it might be found some day bobbing about on the other side of the ocean of space.

Paul: Yes, a very symbolic sort of gesture because the chances of it ever being discovered are infinitesimal.

Phillip: But even if your hypothesis is correct, our symbols, our diagrams, our metaphors, our crude attempts at greetings, might not be intelligible to them at all.

Paul: You see, we're back to chance and necessity. How much of our makeup, you and I, as human beings, is legislated by necessity? How much of it is law-like? How much of it is inevitable? Because to make sense of the world we have to have certain sorts of concepts, certain internal representations of the world, and so on, which we might expect to share with all intelligent beings everywhere. And how much is just an accident of our evolution?

Well, my own personal point of view is that there are certain basic aspects of human nature which are inevitable, given that we have arisen from the law-like order in the universe, and I count mathematics as perhaps the most important of these. The fact that humans can do mathematics, that it applies so well to the physical world –

Phillip: Are you suggesting that this may be a universal language?

Paul: Yes, I am. You see, the laws of nature are mathematical in form. The great book of nature, remarked Galileo, is written in mathematical language. Any species of intelligent beings out there that has developed technology is going to be familiar with these basic mathematical laws of the universe. So that will be the starting point of any dialogue.

Phillip: Paul, you realise that the universal language you speak so fluently is unavailable to many others. I don't speak it and our film crew doesn't either. You're the only person in this remote location who does. I suppose we should take comfort in the thought of you being able to communicate with another species, even if you can't communicate with many of your fellow human beings!

Paul: One of the great tragedies in trying to explain basic physics and cosmology, indeed any science, to the general public is that most people are afraid of mathematics. They don't like it and they don't know much of it, and consequently they are shut off from the language and the poetry of nature.

Phillip: Many people also see it as reductionist. Yet that isn't true of mathematics.

Paul: Absolutely not! There is a feeling that if you can reduce nature to bare formulae this provides a very bleak way of looking at the world. Well, of course it's not bleak, because it is through those formulae that the world comes alive, that you see the subtlety and beauty and harmony of nature that is expressed in this mathematical way.

So mathematics is the universal language – the language of the universe. If there are any aliens – and there may be none, I might say – but if there are any, and if my ideas are correct, then they probably would understand absolutely nothing of our politics, of our music, of our religions and so on, but I think they would understand our mathematics. So any dialogue would have to start on the basis of mathematical exchange.

Phillip: As self-organising processes continue, is it possible, is it likely, is it perhaps even inevitable, that the form of consciousness that we share will deepen and develop?

Paul: It's very hard to say whether humanity is just a transitory phase in the evolution of intelligence on Earth, or whether we are as far as it is going to go. Now, again, if you ask a biologist you'll probably be told that life is unique to Earth, and human intelligence is the best that there is, and we'll probably wipe ourselves out within a few generations and that will be it. The story will end with us. That is a rather sad way of looking at things. But if I am right – that there is this general trend towards greater organisation or complexity – then I would see humanity as just an intermediate step in the general advancement of what we might call mind in the universe, and the influence of mind over the universe.

Phillip: That sounds a bit mystical.

Paul: Let me stress that I'm not talking about anything supernatural here. I'm not talking about mind over matter. All I'm saying is that when human consciousness and human intelligence began to have an impact on the world through technology, we began to reshape this little corner of the universe. We've now reconfigured the surface of our planet. There are pockmarks all around us here at Coober Pedy, evidence of how individuals have changed the landscape in a little way.

Phillip: Whilst looking for opals.

Paul: Quite. But we need only think of the dingo fence down there or the Great Wall of China to see that humans have had an impact on the surface of our planet on a rather large scale. And we could imagine, seeing as there are billions of years before the universe is likely to die, that intelligence and technology can spread out into the universe and bring about enormous changes, changes which would reconfigure not only the surface of a planet, but maybe a whole star system or even an entire galaxy – if we let our imaginations run free!

Phillip: Enough of this frivolity. Let's get back to some good healthy pessimism, and to Herman von Helmholtz. Let us not cavil about it – the second law of thermodynamics is a cosmic death sentence. Tell us how it may be carried out.

Paul: Right. If the universe goes on expanding for ever and ever, as it will if there's not enough matter there to drag it back to a big crunch, then it is a case of death by boredom, really: the slow degeneration of the cosmos over the aeons. The sun, as I've mentioned, will burn out, but only after some billions of years. The galaxy as a whole will start to dim and fade in say, a hundred billion, or a trillion years. After such an immense duration, the whole universe will start to cool and fade. The lights will start going out all around the cosmos.

Phillip: That is the good news, is it?

Paul: That is the good news, because it is by no means the end of the story. It turns out that gravitation, which is ultimately the force responsible for killing all those stars, has within it the power to deliver enormous quantities of useful energy in its own right. Energy sources connected with black holes, for example, that can be tapped by a sufficiently resourceful community – if it can get over the energy crisis of the next trillion years or so! These gravitational processes could in principle extend the longevity of a super-technology for – words fail me – trillions upon trillions upon trillions of years.

But the logic of the second law of thermodynamics is remorseless. However much energy there might be available at the outset, eventually all the sources are going to run down, and it is going to get harder and harder for even the most resourceful, most advanced technological community imaginable to be able to harvest it.

An interesting question therefore arises, one that was extensively investigated by the physicist Freeman Dyson. If the universe goes on expanding for ever – if there is literally an infinite amount of time in the future – but only a finite resource of useful energy, is it possible for a sufficiently resourceful community to nevertheless enjoy an infinite lifetime, by efficiently husbanding and utilising the energy that there is?

It turns out that the answer to this poser depends on the fine details of the physics. It may be yes or no. But it may be possible, if the community hibernates for ever-longer durations, for it to survive for eternity. Indeed, the total amount of active time, integrated over the whole of the future of the universe, might actually be infinite. However, the down time has to get greater and greater. They have to spend an ever-greater fraction of their time in hibernation.

You can imagine these pathetic beings, eking out a desperate existence in the cold and the dark, scavenging –

Phillip: A bit like parliamentary backbenchers.

Paul: It's a bit reminiscent of that . . . scavenging for scraps of energy around the cosmos, and then conserving that energy by going into hibernation for longer and longer periods, really up against it but nevertheless always hanging in there. I must admit it's a very, very bleak vision.

Phillip: I think I'll settle for the giant asteroid!

Paul: Well, I would prefer the big crunch scenario. Remember, this is the theory that the universe reaches a maximum size and then starts to collapse. Well, then it's totally hopeless of course, because in a finite amount of time – maybe billions of years, but certainly a finite amount of time – the entire universe will be crushed and squashed into a single point. All the matter and energy will be obliterated, and space and time will come to an end – time itself will literally stop. The whole show goes off the road at that point. Whichever way you look at it, that is very definitely The End.

iii

The Riddle of Time

Phillip: *The American scientist John Wheeler once described time as that which 'stops everything happening at once'. Of all the Big Questions of existence, perhaps none impacts on our daily lives more than the problem of time. There's never enough of it, of course. Here in the Australian desert, the Dreamtime of the Aborigines collides with the linear time of European culture, leaving both communities puzzled and bewildered. So, can science solve the riddle of time, or are we destined to remain eternally mystified?*

They sometimes call this 'the timeless land', Paul, but of course time is hanging heavy here. We see its commentary on the landscape. It's even making a bit of a commentary on us. So it's time to talk about time. To what extent does time remain an absolute and utter mystery?

Paul: It's not an *utter* mystery, but our personal perception of time is still pretty mysterious, mainly because it doesn't sit easily alongside our understanding of time as achieved through physics. There is a mismatch, a clash; in fact a very violent clash.

Phillip: You're not simply talking Greenwich Mean Time versus Eastern Standard?

Paul: I'm talking about something very deep, which is that in daily life we all have this overwhelming impression that time is *passing*. Time flies, as we say –

Phillip: You're right, Paul, I've noticed that. Unfortunately.

Paul: We have this overwhelming impression that time is in some sense moving, that things change. And our whole language, our entire way of thinking about the world, is rooted in this idea of a *flux* of time. Yet when physicists in the laboratory look to see what causes this flux, when they investigate how we can measure the flux of time, there's nothing there! Time doesn't seem to 'move' or pass at all.

Phillip: Hold on there, Paul. I thought clocks measured the passage of time.

Paul: No, they don't! That's a common fallacy. Clocks measure *intervals* of time, not the *motion of* time; just as rulers measure intervals or distances in space, and not speed or motion *through* space. So I'm not saying that there is no time as such, that time itself is an illusion. Certainly we can measure intervals of time. What we can't measure is the passage of time. Not only can we not measure it, but many philosophers and scientists argue that time simply *doesn't* pass, that our psychological impression of the passage of time is simply an illusion.

Phillip: Well, we have used the term counter-intuitive before, but that is the big one: Counter-Intuitive with capital C and capital I.

Paul: That is the one that had me lying awake in my teens thinking such weird thoughts as: Why am I living now? Why am I me? Is there a future? Does it already exist? What happened to the past?

Phillip: What about your old pal Augustine? Does he have a crack at it in his theology?

Paul: Well, you see, he does, in the sense that he understood the essential riddle. That is why he made his famous statement that we all know what time is until somebody asks us, and then we're lost for words. The point is that time is rather special. It's different from other physical quantities because we *feel* it inside ourselves. Time is in our very souls, isn't it?

Phillip: Well, we have a clock in our chest, don't we, beating away?

Paul: Ah, but it's not just a question of biological rhythms keeping us in tune with our environment. I'm talking about something that we actually feel. The passage of time is something that we can perceive internally, in a way that we can't with intervals of space, or mass, or electric charge; time has this special role. Sir Arthur Eddington, the grand old British astronomer, summed it up quite well by saying it's as if we have 'a back door' into our minds through which nature's temporality creeps. We have a sort of privy view of time, whereas with other physical quantities we have to get at them through our normal senses and external instruments. But time is something that is inside us, and that is why I think people are so fascinated with the nature of time –

Phillip: Fascinated with. And terrified by!

Paul: And terrified, because when scientists start saying such things as 'time is relative', or 'time doesn't pass', or 'time can have a beginning and an end', it seems almost like a personal assault.

Phillip: There was a time when there was only one clock in the village. Up there in the clocktower. And it had only an hour hand. Later the minute hand was added. Then we acquired watches with second hands and you, Paul, have one of those little digital numbers blinking away. As do those fancy atomic clocks. It's as if technological determinism was making life increasingly urgent, more obsessed with time.

Paul: Yes, it wasn't always that way. You see, most ancient cultures didn't have any notion of precision time-keeping in the same way that we have today. They lived very much in tune with the cycles and rhythms of nature, it was almost a biological thing. Curiously enough the Greeks, who did so much to turn geometry into a precise science and art, largely left time alone. It was only with Galileo and Newton, and what we would call the 'scientific revolution', that the notion of time as an infinitely-precisely measurable parameter came into currency. In fact, Newton's own words are 'absolutely true and mathematical time [which] flows equably without relation to anything external'. The notion that time is something 'there', as a sort of backdrop to the universe, slipping by with precise uniformity, stems from Newtonian thought. According to Newton, it's just a matter of refining the technology to be able to measure those time intervals as accurately as we would like.

Phillip: Then along comes the guy with the Harpo Marx haircut – Albert Einstein – and blows that tidy view of time to smithereens!

Paul: That's right, absolutely! Except Einstein was only twenty-six years old when he did it, and the haircut came later. That is the real revolution in our understanding of time, which has taken place in this century. Now, Newton, you see, spoke of time *'flowing* equably'. By extrapolation of common sense and ordinary experience, he assumed that time indeed had this flux, this motion.

Phillip: And he also assumed it could be 'now' everywhere?

Paul: That's right. Newton's time was an absolute and universal time, the *same* time for everybody. According to Newton, your time and my time are exactly the same. It doesn't matter how we move or where we are, there's only one universal time: *the* time.

Well, Einstein demolished that whole set of

ideas. He showed that time is 'relative', to use the jargon. That your time and my time needn't be the same, they can get out of step. In fact, they can get out of step in a very simple way.

Phillip: Well, give us a demonstration of this.

Paul: Yes, well I could, but I'd go off camera, though. All I need to do is to stand up and walk about. That is all I need to do to introduce what we might call a time warp or a time dilation between your time and my time. Ordinary motion is enough!

Phillip: A movement as small as that?

Paul: Well, it would be a very tiny effect. The faster you move the bigger it gets. To see time dilation really conspicuously you would need to go close to the speed of light. Under those circumstances time is very severely distorted, or warped, one relative to the other. But nevertheless, even at everyday speeds it is a measurable effect. So, for example, if you travel in an airliner and take an atomic clock as a passenger, then when you come back to the ground and the clock is compared with its clone left behind at the airport terminal, you will find that there is a measurable discrepancy. It's a real effect, although it's a small effect in the case of aircraft speeds. However, it is measurable; it has actually been measured. I am talking about a few billionths of a second for a few hours' worth of flying, but that is well within the capability of modern atomic clocks.

So time really is warped by motion. And this leads to what is known as the 'twins effect' – sometimes misnamed the twins paradox (it's not actually paradoxical). Imagine a pair of twins, suppose you and I are twins –

Phillip: Hard to imagine, Paul, but I'll struggle to do so!

Paul: – You decide to sit here in Coober Pedy, while I get in my rocket ship over there and head off to a nearby star, close to the speed of light. And you sit here, and sit here, and ten years later you're getting a bit bored, but eventually the rocket ship reappears and out I step. To your astonishment, I don't seem to have aged at all. You say, 'Paul, I've been getting very impatient just sitting here growing old. You've been gone for ten years.' I reply, 'Ten years? Not at all! I've been gone only one year. My watch right here says I've been gone for one year. What's more, I've got a super-accurate chronometer in the rocket ship. It confirms that I really have been gone for only a year.' And looking at me, you have to admit I have aged only very slightly, whereas you are clearly a decade older. We may have been born twins, but apparently we are no longer the same age!

The question raised by this little parable, which Einstein himself alluded to briefly in his first paper on the theory of relativity in 1905, is: who is right? Are you right? Have ten years really elapsed? Or am I right? Has just one year elapsed?

Phillip: Can I ask the question? Who is right?

Paul: Well, the answer is we are both right!

Phillip: I thought you'd say that!

Paul: Because time is relative, your time and my time are different, because we are moving differently. Consequently we measure different intervals of time – ten years and one year respectively – between the *same* two events. And let me stress once again that this is a real effect, not the musings of some mad mathematician. It has actually been observed, though only for small durations in the case of human beings. You can produce dramatically large twins effects using particle accelerators, though. But in this case the twins are subatomic particles.

The twins effect leads to a very profound conclusion about the nature of time because, to return to the Phillip and Paul saga, if having sat here patiently for, say, three years, you then ask the question, 'Well, I wonder what old Davies is doing up there now?' then clearly your question is problematical in my frame of reference. My entire journey is going to take only one year for your ten years. So my now and your now have got out of kilter with each other, just by the simple process of moving differently. What you mean by 'now' after three years and what I mean by 'now' are completely different sets of events.

Phillip: And it would be impossible, of course, to have a Greenwich Mean Time for the entire cosmos.

Paul: That's right! You see, that is the whole point. There can be no absolute and universal time as Newton supposed. Whose time are we going to take for this universal time, this absolute time? Yours? Mine? The sun's? There isn't such a universal time, so the notion of there being a 'universal present moment', or common 'now', throughout the universe – a now which divides time into past, present and future – is clearly meaningless. It's simply been demolished. The experimental evidence shows quite clearly there is no common now.

I should add that it is not just motion that causes a time warp. Gravitation can do it as well. Many people don't realise that clocks tick a little faster in space than they do down here on the surface of the Earth, because Earth's gravity slows time. So if you live at the top of a high-rise building, clocks go a little bit faster than their counterparts at ground level.

Phillip: Does that mean as one approaches a black hole, where gravity is huge, time would stretch almost to the infinite?

Paul: Yes. The surface of a black hole represents an infinite time warp. If we could somehow position a clock on the surface of a black hole – which you can't do, incidentally, but you can imagine it – and if we could observe that clock, it would appear to be frozen in time. In fact, black holes used to be called 'frozen stars' in the old days because time literally stands still there, relative to us here. However, this time dilation is purely relative: the time near the black hole is tremendously stretched out *relative* to Earth time. If you actually went to the surface of the black hole, time there would be exactly as it is anywhere else. You wouldn't notice anything odd about it in your own frame of reference. But comparing clocks there with Earth clocks you would deduce an enormous mismatch.

Phillip: This may be a completely ludicrous question,

but if you were to approach a black hole would your perception of time change?

Paul: No! You see the whole point I am making is that in your own frame of reference time is simply time. It's only by making comparisons between clocks, or personal experiences, in different frames of reference, that you reveal the discrepancies. That is why we say time is relative; your time and my time can be different, relative to each other. But it's not a question of somebody being right and somebody else being wrong.

Phillip: I now have to raise the difficult question – well, for me, impossible – of block time. Let's get back to the idea that time doesn't 'happen'!

Paul: Okay. It was Einstein's colleague Hermann Weyl who said that 'the world doesn't happen, it simply is'. Einstein himself wrote that 'the past, present, and future, are only illusions, however persistent'. Curiously enough, he put that in a letter to the widow of his friend Michel Besso after he died.

Phillip: To console the poor woman?

Paul: Yes.

Phillip: It doesn't sound as though it would have been particularly efficacious.

Paul: Quite. Einstein was implying that in some sense her husband hadn't really passed on, or passed away, because time *doesn't* pass. So the physicist treats time in much the same way as the Greeks treated space; that is, as a dimension. There are three dimensions of space and one dimension of time. Like space, time is simply *there*. It's laid out before us.

I like to use the word 'timescape'. You see, here we sit surrounded by the *landscape*, and there it is! It's laid out before us, all around! Well, if we now regard time as something that is also laid out before us – all at once, so to speak – then that is what I mean by the timescape. It's usually referred to as block time, because it's all there as a single block, rather than as a moment-by-moment moving sequence. That is the way that the physicist thinks about the world and its space-time, as a four-dimensional 'scape'. There are of course events, and there are intervals of time; we use clocks to measure those intervals of time just as we use rulers to measure intervals of space. But nothing's actually *happening*. Space-time – the world – is simply all there at once.

Phillip: Well, Paul, I cannot escape the gravitational pull of my wrist-watch, or the pendulum. But let us imagine that there you are, the god-like physicist, gazing down on this timescape.

There it is. You can see the whole of time. Wouldn't that mean that the universe was predetermined?

Paul: Not necessarily, no. The fact that the future can in some sense already exist is actually not the same thing as saying that the future is completely determined by the present. Determinism means that states of the universe are completely fixed – determined – by earlier states; in other words, that the information needed to deduce, or construct, the future is already contained in the present state of the universe. Now, if the universe *is* deterministic, then a sufficiently god-like intelligence could in principle 'see' the future – by extrapolating from the present. However, it may be that the world is not deterministic. In fact, it almost certainly isn't. Nevertheless, we could still imagine a superbeing who can see the future, and see that it is *not* connected determinstically, rigidly, to the present state. So the two concepts – determinism and knowledge of the future – are logically distinct.

When Einstein said, 'the past, present, and future are only illusions, however persistent', what he meant was that there is nothing in physics to reveal that only the present is real, while the past has somehow slipped away into a half-reality, and the future has yet to come into being. He could make this claim because he realised that there is simply no possibility of chopping up space-time, or the timescape, into this much-discussed 'past, present, and future' in an objective and universal way.

Phillip: Okay, I accept that past, present and future are all equally real.

Paul: Well, if so, they have somehow all got to be there 'at once'. So now the question is, if we think about an event in, I don't know, the year 2100 or something, is that event completely determined by everything that is happening in the universe at this particular time in the year 1995? For that is what determinism means. It means that if you happen to know everything that the universe is doing at one instant, there is enough information there to be able to figure out what it's going to do at some future instant. In Newton's scheme – often called the clockwork universe – nature was indeed treated as a completely deterministic system.

The doctrine of determinism is very profound, because it means that the future in some sense doesn't introduce anything new, that everything about the universe is already contained in its present moment. If the world was like that, then time would be a totally gratuitous thing, just a parameter that fulfils no physical function. It would be just a bookkeeping device; as Wheeler said, stopping everything from happening at once, which would be very confusing!

The Belgian chemist Ilya Prigogine summed it up rather nicely. He remarked that time in a completely deterministic universe would be rather like God turning the pages of a cosmic history book that is already written. There has of late been a bit of a rebellion against the deterministic way of looking at the universe, an attempt to rediscover time in some sense. And discoveries like quantum mechanics and chaos theory mean that few scientists still believe that the universe is strictly deterministic. It's not actually like that.

Phillip: If it is not deterministic, then you'd argue I guess that to some extent the universe has a form of free will?

Paul: Yes, I would say an openness. I don't like the term free will, because I don't really know what it means.

Phillip: You object to the notion when applied to humans?

Paul: Yes, that is correct. What I prefer to do is, rather than trying to find something special about humans that injects this mysterious thing called free will into our actions, I try to find something in the wider universe that can mirror that human freedom. It seems to me that there is a kind of openness in nature in general, an openness to the future, that is present even in inanimate matter.

Phillip: It's there from macro to micro?

Paul: Well, we now know from the theory of chaos, which has been so fashionable in recent years, that even in a system which is in a strict mathematical sense deterministic, nevertheless it is possible for it to still be unpredictable. In a so-called chaotic system, the future behaviour is so exquisitely sensitive to the initial conditions that the slightest change, the slightest error or perturbation, will cause it to do something dramatically different. This is often called the butterfly effect, from the famous example that the mere flap of a butterfly's wings in Coober Pedy today (if there are any butterflies in Coober Pedy!) may change the course of a cyclone off Bali next week. That is because the weather is a chaotic system. So we even know that a system which might be in a strictly mathematical sense deterministic, nevertheless is, for all practical purposes, unpredictable. And human freedom, I think, has something to do with that lack of predictability. The human brain operates at the edge of chaos.

Phillip: Turning now to a completely different but equally baffling temporal topic, what about time travel?

Paul: Ah, yes! Just as we can go to different parts of the landscape, driving around the desert here in our hire car, so we could perhaps visit different parts of the timescape. If the past and future exist, why not? In fact, travel into the future is a reality; we've just been talking about it. The twins effect is essentially time travel into the future. Recall that it is possible for me to go off on a one-year journey as measured in a rocket ship, and to return to you on Earth ten Earth-years later. In that case I have effectively travelled nine years into your future.

Phillip: You would travel into my future?

Paul: In effect, yes. I would have reached Earth-year 2005 in just one year of elapsed time in my frame of reference. But there's a snag. I can't use that method to get back again. I can't just reverse my trajectory in the rocket and come back to the starting point. So time travel into the future, as a one-way journey, is a reality. We can do it. It's been done. We're doing it to a tiny extent all the time by moving about. However, travel into the past is a much tougher proposition.

Phillip: I'd prefer to travel into the past. Personally, I'm more interested in that. Are you going to frustrate my ambitions by telling me I can't go back to ancient Egypt to watch them putting up the pyramids?

Paul: Well, we don't absolutely know that, but it looks to be pretty tough – certainly very expensive! Einstein's theory of relativity, which is about the best thing we have to go on when it comes to the nature of time, leaves open the question as to whether it would be possible to visit the past.

I should explain right at the outset that this is not quite like H.G. Wells' famous story of the time machine where, by throwing a lever on some machine, you can 'make the movie run backwards' and then stop it at some desired stage. Time travel into the past à la Einstein goes a bit like this: you travel around a loop in space and return to your starting place, not at a later time as would be the case for conventional travel, but at a time before you left! Now, that possibility is left open in Einstein's theory, although in practical terms, most of the detailed proposals for actually doing it look to be extremely fanciful, involving wormholes in space or cosmic strings and other hypothetical entities. But we cannot rule out travel into the past at our present state of knowledge.

Phillip: If you could do it, wouldn't it open all sorts of paradoxes?

Paul: Well, it does indeed! I suppose the best known of the time travel paradoxes is the so-called grandfather paradox. Imagine if I were to go back 100 years and seek out my grandfather as a young man and shoot him, what then would happen? If poor old Grandad is dead then Paul Davies would never have been born; but then Paul Davies could never become a time traveller. So I couldn't have gone back to commit the murder after all. But if Grandad isn't murdered I *will* be born . . . and so on. We get inconsistent nonsense. This is always the problem with travel into the past – as opposed to the future – because the past is connected to the present (and future) through causality. If we go back and change the past we change the present as well, and that is a really major problem for the whole idea of travel into the past. For that reason and others, Stephen Hawking introduced what he called the 'chronology protection hypothesis' – making the universe safe for historians. The hypothesis states that in some way nature must prevent us from travelling back into the past, even if it appears that the laws of physics will allow us to do it.

Phillip: But haven't I heard somewhere that if the universe decides to collapse back to a big crunch –

along the lines we were discussing earlier – that time would run backwards?

Paul: That is a different state of affairs. Travelling backwards in time, and time *itself* reversing, may sound similar but they're actually logically different. You are right that it has often been conjectured that the arrow of time may turn around in a contracting universe.

Phillip: Explain what you mean by the arrow of time.

Paul: I mean the fact that we see sequences of events all around us in nature that have a definite directionality to them. In our last discussion we talked about the second law of thermodynamics, which says that the universe is irreversibly running down, the stars are burning out, people grow old, eggs break, and so on. These are one-way-in-time processes: we don't see them go backwards. We can think of the direction 'past-future' as denoted by an arrow; the arrow of time. The arrow metaphor doesn't imply that time is *flowing* from past to future – I've been at pains to refute that idea – it is more like a compass arrow, indicating a direction rather than a motion.

We started out by talking about the timeless landscape, but of course it's not really timeless. If you took a movie film of that scene behind us, then over a few million years you'd certainly notice changes. And if you ran that movie film in reverse we'd all spot that it was running backwards. Conjectures about time running backwards are a little bit like saying that it is possible under some circumstances for the great cosmic movie, as it were, to run in reverse; for rivers to flow uphill, for broken eggs to reassemble themselves, for people to grow younger instead of older. It's a very appealing idea – a very ancient idea that goes right back to early Greece. Plato himself wrote graphically about this scenario.

Phillip: And Thomas Gold and Stephen Hawking do now!

Paul: That's right. The notion has been resurrected in its modern form by a number of people. In the 1960s Thomas Gold suggested that the arrow of time – the directionality of physical processes – has something to do with the expansion of the universe. In other words, the fact that the universe is growing bigger every day somehow drives all these irreversible processes in the direction of greater entropy. Gold then reasoned that if the universe should start to shrink in size again, at some later stage in its evolution, then the arrow of time would reverse, and things would tend to run backwards.

Gold quickly spotted that if there were any intelligent beings around in this collapsing phase of the universe they wouldn't notice anything unusual. They wouldn't say, 'Good heavens, everything's running backwards! I can remember tomorrow and predict yesterday,' because of course their mental processes would also be reversed, so they would regard their phase of the universe as perfectly normal. They would see, through their reversed-time eyes and reversed-time brains, the universe expanding. From their point of view it would be *us* who lived in a contracting universe, and *our* physical and mental processes that ran backwards.

Phillip: It raises tantalising possibilities for the punter, doesn't it?

Do you think we are about to have one of those paradigm shifts that you've been describing, in regard to time? Given that Einstein's ideas are now getting pretty elderly, it's remarkable how little effect this has had on ordinary people who still insist that time's winged heels –

Paul: It is astonishing! I've recently written a book on time, and been travelling around the world giving lectures on the subject, talking about things which have been pretty standard stuff for physics undergraduates for decades, results which are now nearly a century old. Yet people are still absolutely astonished to learn of things like the twins effect.

Phillip: Well, the trickle-down effect is going to take more time, isn't it? But you're right. We hold on to our old-fashioned concept of time because it's built into us!

Paul: We have still got this essentially Newtonian view of the universe, of time that is absolute and universal. People give that up very reluctantly, because in daily life we don't notice these weird time warps. But if we could move at close to the speed of light or through intense gravitational fields we'd become very familiar with Einstein's time.

Phillip: And will that ever happen, do you think? Projecting into the future – following the arrow – do you think our technologies will one day allow us to travel at near the speed of light?

Paul: Not in our lifetime!

Phillip: You have based most of what you are claiming about time on Einstein's work. Yet he wasn't infallible. Didn't he make what he himself called his 'greatest mistake' in relation to time?

Paul: Yes, he did. This is a curious story concerned with the age of the universe – the time that has elapsed since the big bang. We were talking earlier about a discrepency between the age of the universe and the ages of the stars – the oldest stars. Let me remind you that the oldest stars seem to be about fourteen or fifteen billion years old, but the best guess at the age of the universe, based on the Hubble telescope data, gives it an age of perhaps no more than ten or twelve billion years.

Shortly after Einstein had generalised his theory of relativity in 1915, he constructed a mathematical model of the universe with it. In those days nobody knew the universe was expanding, so Einstein assumed that on a large scale the cosmos would be static and eternal. This model of Einstein's is actually very strange, I might say, because he was thoroughly familiar with the second law of thermodynamics, and surely could have figured that the stars can't have been burning for all eternity. Yet he went ahead and tried to find, within his general theory of relativity, a way of making the universe static and infinitely old.

Now, in cosmology, the only force in town is gravitation. Gravitation is a pulling force, an attractive force. And therefore, if you have a static universe and let it go, it will inevitably collapse under gravity – collapse in on itself to a big crunch. If you wanted the universe to be static you would have to combat that attractive force of gravity with an opposing repulsive force. Well, that is just what Einstein proposed. He introduced into his theory of relativity a repulsive form of gravity – anti-gravity if you like – to balance the attraction of the gravitational force.

Phillip: Did the idea work?

Paul: Not very well. One problem was that the balancing act was unstable. It only needed for someone to sneeze and the entire universe would either collapse to a big crunch or head off on a runaway expansion! More to the point, Einstein discovered to his chagrin in 1931 that the universe isn't really static anyway – it's expanding. Because he had been so preoccupied with trying to explain how a universe could be static, he'd missed the chance to conclude that perhaps it isn't static, but expanding. He could have actually predicted the expansion of the universe if he'd stuck to his guns and kept with the original formulation of the theory, without the added extra of the repulsive force.

Phillip: That was his great mistake?

Paul: That was his greatest mistake, yes. He dropped the cosmic repulsion idea in disgust, calling it the greatest blunder of his career. But now we encounter a twist of irony. In recent years the cosmic repulsion force has made a bit of a comeback. It now turns out that some sort of cosmic repulsion, some sort of anti-gravity, is an almost inevitable by-product of the other forces of nature, for example the nuclear forces. So what Einstein threw out of the front door has come back in through the window.

Phillip: How does the anti-gravity force help with the age-of-the-universe problem?

Paul: The reason that this repulsion force can fix up the time scale discrepancy is because it affects the way in which the expansion of the universe changes with time. Remember that the universe starts out expanding explosively fast in the big bang, but progressively slows, as gravity acts like a brake on the expansion rate? Well, just as normal attractive gravity brakes the expansion, so anti-gravity accelerates it. So if both forces act together, it's rather like driving a car with your foot on both the brake and accelerator pedals at the same time.

By reducing the braking effect, Einstein's anti-gravity force alters the relationship between the present rate of expansion of the universe and the inferred age. The more anti-gravity you have, the older the universe will be for a given rate of expansion today. So my preferred resolution of the age-of-the-universe discrepancy is that Einstein was right all along. If so, then his greatest mistake could yet turn out to be his greatest triumph!

iv

The Ghost in the Machine

Phillip: *Ever since Descartes pronounced, 'I think therefore I am', consciousness has been regarded as the most fundamental aspect of existence. After all, no consciousness, and there's nobody around to notice the rest of the world. But what is consciousness and how has it evolved? Do minds really exist or are they just a by-product of language?*

Paul, we talked about time as something that people feel innately – they feel the passage of time. The other thing that people feel innately is their own existence. They are conscious of their own consciousness, they are aware of themselves, of being alive. Maybe we are unique in this ability. But this is deep into the territory of philosophy and psychology. What can the physicist tell us about consciousness?

Paul: From the point of view of the physicist, consciousness is a very mysterious phenomenon. First of all, we would like to know what consciousness is for, so to speak. That is, what role it plays in nature. Secondly, how does it arise? What physical processes produce it?

There is a whole set of questions revolving around what is known as the mind-body problem. Let me explain the essence of the problem in the following way. From the physicist's point of view the mystery is this: I think thoughts, I have ideas, emotions, impressions, sensations – mental activity – and I can respond to this mental activity in a very obvious way, just by moving parts of my body. So, for example, if I would like to raise my arm to wave away a fly ... my arm obligingly goes up.

Now, how can thoughts do that? How can the desire 'I would like to raise my arm' be turned into the physical activity of the arm moving? Well, we can trace back a sort of chain of command, can't we? We know that there are nerve impulses in my arm that cause the muscles to contract, and these nerve impulses have travelled down my nerve fibres from my brain, so the signals originate in electrical activity in my brain. But what is it that just triggers all that, that chain of command? What starts those electric currents off in the first place? How is it that a thought can be translated into electrons moving down nerves and so on? (Actually, it's a lot more complicated than electrons moving, but never mind.) To put it in the most blunt form, how can *thoughts* move matter?

There is a flip side to this problem, which is how electrical activity can create thoughts, or sensations, or desires, or whatever. Take the sensation of seeing something. For example, light strikes my eye and turns into an electrical impulse in my optic nerve, and those signals get amplified and enter my brain, and patterns of electrical activity then swirl around my brain as a result. Well, how can those patterns of electrical activity create the sensation of sight?

What we are trying to do here is to dovetail the mental world – the world of ideas, thoughts, emotions, sensations and so on – into the physical world, the world of electrons (or whatever) moving according to the laws of physics, and arms that brush away flies. How can we fit these totally different worlds – the mental and the physical – together? That's the problem!

Phillip: Paul, I am aware that almost every branch of science seems to be attacking the problem of consciousness – there's a profusion of books and theories coming out. But where are you physicists?

Paul: Floundering around, I think! There are some scientists who think that consciousness is such a problem it is best defined away. Let's sweep it under the carpet, they say. Let's make out that the conscious self doesn't really exist, that we only imagine it – we merely hallucinate our own existence. Then the problems go away. Thoughts can't move electrons or arms or whatever, because there *are* no thoughts – at least, there are no thoughts that are *things* with physical efficacy; there are only electrons and other matter frolicking about in accordance with physical laws.

So there is a strong temptation to try and define the problem away, to say that the human body or the human brain is just a very complicated machine, doing what all machines do, which is slavishly complying with the laws of physics. In that case, if you knew enough about what's going on in my head you could predict precisely what I'm going to do. Any notion of there being a self in my head here, a self which has a certain will, wanting to move an arm, and so on, just disappears. I am reduced to a very complicated machine.

Phillip: Sorry, that's not acceptable in this context. You will have to do better than that!

Paul: It seems to be unacceptable because our most primitive experience is of our own existence. We can directly perceive that we exist. I *know* that I exist, and whilst I can't be absolutely sure that there is anybody at home over there – any conscious being inside Phillip Adams, that is – I can't be sure that you are not some incredibly cleverly programmed automaton, a zombie. I do nevertheless know that *I* am not a zombie!

Phillip: Yes, but I don't know that!

Paul: No! That's right! The problem here is that we infer the existence of other minds, of other consciousnesses, by analogy. I observe that you behave in a manner similar to me, so it seems reasonable to suppose that there is a conscious, feeling being inside your body. If I stamp on your toe and you scream, I imagine that you feel pain.

Phillip: That's preordained by the laws of physics?

Paul: No. What is preordained by the laws of physics are the nerve impulses and the other activities going on in your brain, but as for the actual *feeling* part, physics doesn't seem to be able to say anything.

Phillip: Let's get back to the question that you raised earlier. What role does consciousness play? What is its advantage?

Paul: This is the mystery if we try to define it away, for then why do we possess it (or imagine we possess it) at all? In other words, if a cleverly programmed automaton, or a zombie, that had evolved to perform a lot of complicated functions, can get by in the world without being conscious of its own existence, what is the purpose of us having this consciousness or this self-consciousness, this self-awareness? It does seem to be a mystery if it doesn't fulfil any useful role in nature. So I think we have to take consciousness seriously, in spite of the fact that many scientists would like to do away with it.

Phillip: Well, let's flip it over and look at it from another view. A non-scientific viewpoint. Consciousness is clearly a two-edged sword because, whilst it appears to help us in dealing with existential problems, it makes us pay a terrible price. It gives us an awareness of our mortality. It gives us suffering as well as joy. It is not an unalloyed pleasure to possess consciousness.

Paul: No, indeed not! A lot of people try to argue that human beings are the only ones who are fully aware of their own existence, and indeed their own mortality. We might be satisfied that Phillip Adams isn't a zombie, but what about a cat or a dog? Or a cockroach? It's very hard to say just by looking at the behaviour of animals whether they are truly conscious of their own existence, or whether they are like very sophisticated computers.

If you live with a cat or a dog it's very tempting to suppose that they are fully conscious of their own existence, so that when the dog chases after a rabbit or digs up a bone it seems to have desires, purposes – at least some internal representation of the world: 'I would like to get at that bone, and I'm going to go out and dig it up!' You could believe it. But then there are other examples of animal behaviour where it seems to be, as some people like to say, 'purely instinctual'. The animal is behaving in a certain way that may superficially look intelligent and knowing, but is actually reminiscent of an automaton carrying out a ritual activity without being aware of what it is doing. And there doesn't seem to be a noticeable dividing line between these different sorts of behaviour, which has led some people to claim that *all* animal actions are machine-like.

Phillip: But you would have to extend that to many of our own activities as human beings?

Paul: Yes, that's right, which is another powerful argument deployed by the consciousness-isn't-real brigade. It's undeniably true that most of the things we do in life we don't really give a thought to – walking, breathing, eating –

Phillip: Driving a car becomes an acquired skill. We do it without much thought.

Paul: Driving a car, yes! Even talking. I found it an extraordinary thing that when our children were small, I could sit there of an evening and read a story to them; the words would all come out right, including the inflection – the whole thing would make sense – and yet I wasn't taking any of it in because I was thinking about some physics problem! What a terrible confession! And so one part of our brains can process information about children's stories and speaking, whilst another part is doing something else like mathematics. So you can't tell just from the behaviour of something – however clever it may appear to be – that there's somebody at home, that there's something conscious going on inside.

Phillip: Let us accept that consciousness is real. Can you deduce some practical evolutionary purpose for our degree of it?

Paul: It's easy to use consciousness-type language to

see an advantage. For example, it is clearly advantageous to be able to predict the future to a limited extent – to plan. Supposing we were stranded here in this very hostile environment. It would be necessary to find water, and I might want to say, 'Well, you look over there and I'll look over here. We'll meet up again at that hill this time tomorrow.' In order to make those sorts of plans, to act in cooperation, to have social activity, to be able to think ahead, you need to have some concept of your own existence, the existence of other people and of the natural world, not to mention durations of time, and so on. So looking at it in the way that we do when we make such plans in daily life, consciousness seems to be a very useful thing. But then we can see other animals apparently doing similar things, executing strategies, cooperating and so on – animals that the biologists tell us are either not aware of their own existence, or at any rate do not have such a developed sense of consciousness as we do; migrating birds, for example.

Phillip: Or a lion pack attacking, the way they coordinate their activities?

Paul: Exactly! So it's very hard to know precisely where consciousness comes in.

Phillip: Both of us enjoy from time to time reading

Oliver Sacks' works, and one of his studies concerns someone who, because of brain damage, lives in a constant now.

Paul: It's quite clear to me that the nature of consciousness or, let me phrase it slightly differently, the nature of selfhood, and the nature of time, are very closely interwoven. I don't think we'll solve the one problem without solving the other, because when we talk about the self as an entity what we mean is something that is preserved through time.

You know, it's a very curious thing about the self, that it is a paradoxical mixture of something which is unchanged with time and something that changes with time. If you ask, 'Are you the same person you were at the age of ten?' well, in one sense you are; there's a continuity of memory, certain personality traits remain unchanged, and so on. On the other hand, you are clearly not exactly the same person. Not only has your body changed but your mind has changed as well. So there is something that we like to call the 'self' which is preserved intact through time, and yet something in there is changing, too. So I don't think we are ever going to understand what we mean by the self without understanding the psychology of temporality and the puzzle of the sensation of the flux of time.

Phillip: With Alzheimer's disease we often observe the person's physicality, even some vestige of personality traits, but the self gradually evaporates.

Paul: So it would appear. It's quite clear that consciousness – selfhood – and mental activity in general, are very intimately connected with the electrochemical activity of the brain. I make this obvious point because there are some people who adhere to a theory called panpsychism, according to which consciousness is somehow spread throughout the whole universe. It is not confined to brains. Panpsychists maintain that every little particle of matter is conscious. Even atoms are a little bit conscious. Then all that happens in the brain is that in some way the complicated assemblage of matter there amplifies this all-pervasive consciousness. If that view is correct, which I find it hard to believe, then even a rock is a little bit conscious. This gives some people a sort of respect for the environment, Mother Earth, the wider cosmos, and so on.

Phillip: It's the basis of many an animist faith. In Bali people believe that this tree and that rock have some rudimentary form of consciousness.

Paul: I think it's a load of nonsense, frankly. From the scientific point of view consciousness is associated with complexity, and the brain is an exceedingly complex system. In my opinion, consciousness *emerges* when matter and energy are organised to a certain level of complexity. So it is entirely possible, although I don't know the answer to this, that human beings are unique in having the required level of complexity for full self-awareness to emerge.

Phillip: Could we replicate, down the track, this level of complexity in our gizmos? Will we achieve, do you imagine, a genuine artificial *consciousness* to go with artificial intelligence?

Paul: A lot of people think that if we could build a sufficiently advanced computer, then that computer would be conscious, having wishes and hopes and fears and feelings, and so on. I'm sceptical that the sorts of devices that we call computers at the moment could actually achieve consciousness. However it's perfectly clear to me that if consciousness is associated with a physical process of some sort – swirling electrical patterns, say – as exemplified in complex brain activity, then we could in principle build a system that would be conscious. It's quite obvious, for example, that if we could map your body and brain to a sufficient level of detail and build a replica over here then we would have something that is conscious. We can imagine rebuilding or duplicating Phillip

Adams atom by atom, ending up with a conscious person.

It's very important to realise that every atom in your body – imagine plucking a carbon atom out of your brain, for example – is identical to a carbon atom in a lump of wood, or a carbon atom in the sun, or whatever. Carbon atoms are all precisely identical, so there is nothing special about the *stuff* of which you are made. It is the way that stuff is put together that is the key to producing life and consciousness. It is the complex organisation of the matter that gives rise to consciousness, not the actual material of which you are made.

There is an old concept, often dubbed 'the ghost in the machine', that goes back to the seventeenth-century French scientist and philosopher René Descartes, who proposed that there are two kinds of substance or thing in the world. First, there is ordinary matter, the good old sort of concrete stuff. Secondly, there is 'mind-stuff'. Descartes believed that both brains and minds are physical things – different sorts of things, to be sure: brains are made of ordinary matter, and minds are supposed to be made of some mysterious, etherial, nebulous sort of substance. Descartes had this idea that minds attach themselves to brains and control them by exerting subtle physical forces. This theory, which became known as dualism because there are two different things – minds and brains – at work together, is rather like driving a car. We can think of our bodies and brains as just like machines, like a car, for example, with the mind somehow attaching itself to this vehicle and steering it, in the manner of a driver steering a car. From such analogies, the dualist theory of Descartes' was later described as 'the ghost in the machine'.

This type of imagery – that a human being consists of two components: a body and a mind (or a soul, if you prefer) – has taken root. A lot of popular conceptions of the soul in religion derive from this Cartesian view – the view of Descartes'. You can understand the appeal, of course, of the mind or soul being some sort of nebulous substance that attaches itself to your head, or floats just above your head, or something.

Phillip: Especially as those theologies also allow for the removal of the ghost from the machine entirely, so you can have the ghost minus the machine, or independent from the machine. That means after the machine is dead the ghost goes on!

Paul: That's right, that's the appeal of this 'ghost in the machine' imagery, that when the machine dies, the disembodied ghost can float away to somewhere else. But I might say that the notion of the self, or the soul, or the mind, as some sort of independent thing – a nebulous substance that attaches itself to a body – does not have a long history in Judaism and Christianity. You can't find many references to those sorts of ideas in the Bible.

Anyway, dualism à la Descartes makes very little sense at all from the point of view of science. Firstly, it doesn't really solve any problems, because if you're trying to explain human behaviour in terms of the mind – that is, trying to figure out why the machine behaves in the way it does in terms of a hypothetical 'driver' – you're just pushing back the problem one step. You then have to explain how the driver, or ghost, itself works, what laws it obeys, and so on.

Phillip: And you also have to explain the enormous variety of ghosts in apparently similar machines. One ghost writes *Hamlet*, another ghost comes up with $E=mc^2$.

Paul: An even greater problem is, where do these ghosts come from? Who supplies them and how do they glue themselves on to the machine? The really major stumbling block for this dualist or Cartesian view of the ghost in the machine is this: if minds are things made of stuff, we can ask what size and shape they are. Do they have sharp edges? Spikes? Can they bump into each other and bounce off again? Do they attach themselves to all of the brain, or several small parts, or one part? And how exactly do minds steer brains? What forces do they deploy to move atoms about?

It all seems absurd and unworkable, and so the idea grew up that minds (or souls) are not actually located in space at all. But then we have the worse problem of how it is that something which is not in space can interact with something that is. How can something which isn't anywhere move a material particle that is? How can a molecule in a brain cell, moving along a certain trajectory, get nudged to one side by this nebular stuff called mind, which isn't situated anywhere definite? So this whole dualistic view really fell apart, because no convincing explanation could be given of the interaction between the mind and the brain.

To summarise, I would make the following two points that (a) – I think we have to take consciousness seriously. I think it is something that really exists and has a real role to play in nature. It is not just an illusion, something that we could sweep under the carpet, and (b) – we really don't know, on the basis of our present understanding of physics, how consciousness works or is associated with matter in any very convincing way.

Phillip: Is there not another problem, too, about consciousness, that gets us into the difficulty over the observer and the observed?

Paul: In a way, the problem of the observer and the observed is the oldest problem of philosophy – and indeed, of science. For most of the history of science the observer was pushed out of the picture. In Newton's physics, for example, the observer is just an onlooker, just that. Although in practice, of course, every time we make an observation of the world we inevitably interact with it, interfere with it, disturb it in some way. However, in Newton's scheme this disturbance can be reduced to as little as you like.

Let me give you a simple example. Suppose I want to measure the temperature of a glass of water. I put the thermometer into the water and wait for a little bit, then read off the temperature. Well, the very act of putting the thermometer in the water will change the temperature I'm trying to measure, because the thermometer will absorb some heat.

Now, in the old-fashioned way of looking at

such situations, it was always possible to imagine a very refined experiment in which you could either reduce this disturbance to something of negligible proportions, or you could cleverly allow for it in your results. Then in the early part of this century our entire view of nature was transformed with something called quantum physics, or quantum mechanics. The essence of quantum mechanics is that there is an *irreducible* disturbance that takes place whenever a microscopic system is observed. (By a microscopic system I mean something of atomic or molecular proportions.) Thus, down at the scale of atoms and molecules, the very act of observation disturbs a system in a way that simply cannot be reduced to zero or allowed for in any predictable way. This means that the disturbance is irretrievably part of the measurement process.

As a result of these inescapable disturbances, the observer and the observed became entangled – intertwined – in a way that is simply inherent in nature at the most fundamental level and irreducible even in principle. And so we are presented with a major problem – how to relate observer and observed – but also a major opportunity. The major opportunity is that here, for the first time in physics, we see notions of *observation* (equals mind) entering in physics at a very fundamental level, and not just in an incidental, onlooking capacity. So this is a loophole that could *just* provide the clue to explaining consciousness within the scope of physics.

Phillip: The Oxford mathematician Roger Penrose, who is someone with whom you agree and disagree quite passionately, has argued that quantum physics acts in the brain and is somehow creating consciousness.

Paul: Yes, he has. Now there is a danger in using the following argument: that the act of observation in quantum mechanics is a mystery, consciousness is a mystery; therefore one explains the other. It could just be that we've got two quite separate mysteries. However, it makes sense at least to explore the way in which quantum physics might have a role to play in the brain. At first sight this doesn't seem very promising, because the brain is a pretty big system compared to the size of an atom. Even individual neurons in the brain are enormous compared to atomic and molecular sizes. So it seems very hard to see how quantum effects – which are very prominent at the atomic level – can have any effect at all at the level of neurons, still less on the macroscopic patterns swirling around in the brain.

Before dismissing Penrose's claim, however, I

think it's very important to see if there might be ways in which these subtle quantum effects could become amplified. There is a classic example we know where amplification can take place: the superconductor. If you cool certain metals close to absolute zero, perfect electrical current can flow. The explanation lies with quantum mechanics. Now, a superconductor can be big – centimetres in size, for example – yet it still manifests quantum effects. Zillions of electrons organise themselves to form a very coherent pattern of flow through the superconductor. Maybe something like that is happening in the brain, but we really don't know.

Phillip: To what extent is consciousness driven, or made possible, or even limited, by language? I include in that the language of mathematics. Can you imagine a consciousness that is not articulate?

Paul: It's often said that our awareness of our own existence – this concept of selfhood – is intimately tied up with our use of language, and that if we didn't have language we wouldn't really feel that each of us had an independent existence. This is one of those unanswerable questions, because supposing you came upon a being who was conscious of her or his own existence, or its own existence, but they couldn't tell you about it! Well, how would you know they were aware of themselves? How would you know what's going on in there? So there is something about the very nature of the problem, as you've stated it, that makes it unanswerable. I've always been sceptical about the view that self-identity depends on the use of language – that all it is that makes me aware of my own existence is my ability to tell you about it.

Phillip: The first time I heard the term 'ghost in the machine' wasn't in a treatise on Descartes, but in a book by Arthur Koestler who, you'll recall, had left the Communist Party – and its rigid belief system – to flounder around in religion and metaphysics and the paranormal. Although we promised to leave the discussion of religion until last, I recall Koestler suggesting that the universe was behaving like 'a great thought'. You previously suggested that the future isn't fixed – that nothing is predetermined in minute detail. Instead, your universe, like Koestler's, could be seen as 'trying ideas out'. We've just been discussing the nature of mind primarily in relation to human beings. But if the universe really is in some sense 'trying ideas', then are you willing to entertain the possibility that there may be an *ultimate* consciousness?

Paul: I've made it very clear that I think that consciousness is something associated with complexity, and therefore that I wouldn't expect to find a rock to be conscious, or for that matter a star or a planet. Consciousness seems to be something that emerges over time as complexity advances. So it's very hard for me to see how there could be consciousness in the universe just after the big bang, for example, when everything was very hot and dense but also very simple.

Now I do agree with Koestler (and it was also stated by the Bristish astronomer Sir James Jeans) that the universe is like a great thought. There is a suggestion in the ingenuity of the laws of nature that there has been some intellectual input. Nature is a manifestation of something rational and clever. But you have to be very careful in interpreting these concepts. When I use language like 'I see the need for some intellectual input in explaining the world', or 'there is something like meaning or purpose in the universe', I don't mean to convey the impression that this is like some sort of disembodied super-mind floating about the cosmos performing miracles. Many people have that image. To me, the idea that some super-intelligence, or super-consciousness, is moving stars and planets around, and was doing so before humans came on the scene, I find ridiculous. It is far too crude. We need something deeper, more subtle. But we shall be talking again about this later.

V

In Search of the Theory of Everything

Phillip: *All science can be seen as a search for unity. By discovering deep linkages between different physical phenomena, scientists can construct simpler yet more powerful descriptions of reality. The subject of subatomic particle physics is full of these unifying connections. But how far can this process go? Can we envisage a final theory that brings together all things in a single mathematical scheme, or is this pure intellectual arrogance?*

Paul, the end of the day approaches, along with the end of the century, and indeed the millennium. Millenarian and Apocalyptic theories abound. I've recently interviewed a number of men who insist that they are the Messiah. Meanwhile, academics tell me it's the end of history, and others that it's the end of ideology. Are we, perhaps, reaching the end of physics?

Paul: The science of physics in its broadest sense is 2500 years old. In its modern form it dates from the time of Isaac Newton and is three centuries old. Where are we at after all those years of endeavour? Well, there is a feeling abroad in the physics community that we are approaching some sort of culmination, some sort of drawing together of the threads. I am the first to admit that that may be an illusion. It may be that in another ten or twenty years the convergence of knowledge that we glimpse today will all fall apart again. However, I believe that at least part of our understanding of the world – the microscopic part – is converging towards a type of unified theory.

Phillip: Let me prevent premature ejaculation on this issue and ask you for a potted history of the sequence of events. It's usually a good idea to go back to the Greeks.

Paul: The idea of unifying knowledge – unifying our understanding of the physical world – is a very ancient one, dating at least from the early Greek philosophers. They puzzled over such things as the relationship between permanence and change, and being and becoming. They were baffled as to how some things seem to change while other things appear to remain the same. They tied themselves up into philosophical knots by worrying about the nature of identity. Everything is what it is, they reasoned. So how can A ever change into B, if B is not A?

There were two schools of thought about whether change or permanence was the more fundamental attribute. Is everything ultimately mutable, or is there really nothing new under the sun? Both seemed unsatisfactory. Then along came the Atomists with a neat solution. The idea of atomism is that beneath the complexity and diversity of physical forms and systems that we see around us in the universe, lies a pleasing and harmonious simplicity. Everything in the physical world is put together out of a few simple basic building blocks, so the differences between things is attributed solely to the different arrangements of building blocks within them. Also, everything that ever happens in the universe is simply the rearrangement of these building blocks.

The Greeks called the basic building blocks 'atoms'. At the time there was no way they could check this hypothesis. It took two thousand years before science began to provide ways of examining matter on a sufficiently microscopic scale. Then evidence for these atoms started to emerge. And now, in the twentieth century, we finally believe that there are things called atoms. However, the objects we call atoms today are not the elementary building blocks of the ancient Greeks. The essential property of the Greek atoms was that they should be indestructible and primitive – truly primitive in the sense there were no bits inside of them, no component parts. The things we call atoms today we can break apart. They are composite bodies with internal parts, such as a nucleus. The nucleus itself contains neutrons and protons, and even these particles are not truly elementary, but composed of smaller entities called quarks. So there is a sort of hierarchy.

Phillip: Paul, there used to be a belief that we might be dealing with infinite regress here. Has that notion been disposed of once and for all?

Paul: I don't think you can dispose of the idea of infinite regress, because at any given time science can probe only to a certain scale of size. At the moment we can look at structure on scales of about one-thousandth of the size of an atomic nucleus – perhaps a bit smaller than that – but if we could get down to some smaller size still we might discover a whole new world of complexity. Now, there is a sort of act of faith among physicists that as you break matter apart and get down to smaller and smaller scales of size, things ought to get simpler and simpler.

I might say, just as an historical note, I can well remember that when I was a student in the 1960s it was a rather bad time for this whole program. Atoms had been well known for many decades. The existence of the nucleus and the neutrons and protons had been known for thirty or forty years, but there seemed to be a huge and bewildering proliferation of other subatomic entities, created by the so-called atom smashers. These particle-accelerator machines were churning out new particles almost monthly. Physicists soon ran out of names for them, so they had to invent Greek letters and so on. So all these particles were appearing and nobody had a clue as to what they all were or how they all fitted together. It resembled a zoo, and one could imagine that there was going to be an unlimited number of varieties of particles as you got more and more into matter. Then slowly some order began to appear. It was discovered that many of these different types of subatomic splinters were actually related to each other like members of a family.

Phillip: Are you talking about the forces now between them?

Paul: No, I'm talking about the actual identities of the particles. There was this whole shopping list of particles, so to speak. At first nobody knew quite what to do with them. Then physicists discovered that if they measured certain properties, like mass, or electric charge, or spin, the particles could be grouped together into families according to these properties. At this point some very clever people spotted that the relationships between the members of these families were actually certain abstract mathematical symmetries.

Symmetry has played a very important part in our attempt to understand nature. We see examples of geometrical symmetry all around us in the physical world; think of the spherical figure of the sun or the hexagonal pattern of a snowflake. But the symmetries of the subatomic realm are of an abstract nature, so they can only be expressed mathematically. However, they are very distinctive.

Well then, instead of there being just a sort of random and arbitrary collection of different types of animals down there at the subatomic level, it turned out there was a hidden order of a subtle mathematical nature having to do with these symmetries. However, there were gaps in these patterns, gaps that looked as inelegant as a missing tooth. One of the fascinating things about this subject is the way the gaps get filled – the missing tooth turns up!

Again if I may allude back to the time when I was a student, many particles had been discovered and arranged into these pretty patterns, with hints of underlying symmetries. Then some bright physicists, such as Murray Gell-Mann, looked at the gaps in the patterns and predicted that there ought to be such-and-such a particle to go in that gap, with a certain mass, electric charge, and so on. And of course the experimenters went out and looked for these particles. Lo and behold, there they were! A marvellous example of the rationality of nature.

Phillip: Tell us now about the four fundamental forces that operate at the subatomic level.

Paul: Well, all these particles of matter don't just go about their business in isolation, they interact with each other. There are four distinct forces that physicists recognise as being basic forces of nature. Two of these forces are familiar in daily life. There's gravitation: if we drop an object it falls to the ground. So gravity is a force we recognise in daily life. Then there's electromagnetism. Now, I should mention that 200 years ago electricity was one force, magnetism was another. They were regarded as separate phenomena. Then the work of Michael Faraday, James Clerk Maxwell, and others in the nineteenth century, suggested that electricity and magnetism were in fact closely interwoven. Electricity can produce magnetism, magnetism can produce electricity. Maxwell showed that electricity and magnetism are in fact two components of a single, unified *electromagnetic* force. So now we talk of electromagnetism as a single force, but it was the first example of the unification of two forces into one.

To summarise: we have gravitation, we have electromagnetism. Then in this century physicists have discovered two more forces, the so-called nuclear forces, which are simply called 'weak' and 'strong'. There's a weak nuclear force and a strong nuclear force. So there are now four forces: gravitation, electromagnetism and the weak and strong nuclear forces.

Phillip: And they are crying out for a grand unified theory?

Paul: That's right! If electricity and magnetism can be parts of a single electromagnetic force, why can't these other forces be brought into the scheme and unified, too? In fact, as long ago as the 1830s Michael Faraday performed an experiment at the Royal Institution in London in which he tried to discover whether there was a link between electricity and gravitation. He foresaw that there may be some sort of deep amalgamation possible, but unfortunately he didn't discover it. It was an idea that sort of faded away but has now come back into vogue.

What happened was that in the late 1960s Abdus Salam in Britain and Steven Weinberg in America discovered a mathematical formulation that seemed to describe the electromagnetic force and the weak nuclear force as part of a single scheme. Their ideas were later tested experimentally and found to be correct. After that, many people tried to find an even more embracing theory that would merge the strong force with the unified electromagnetic-weak force. There are several proposed schemes that will do this, but so far the experiments have failed to yield any evidence of a link. The final step would be to bring in gravitation, too, and again there is a theory that seems to do that, but it is far too soon to know whether this completely unified theory of the forces will be completely successful.

There is a feeling among some physicists that if we were to live in a world with, say, four or three truly fundamental forces, then that would be a bit arbitrary! You know, why four rather than fourteen? It would be much easier to have one underlying superforce, or masterforce, that manifests itself in four different varieties according to circumstances.

Phillip: Now, am I right in suspecting that there are some people who want to tie all this up with string, that is, these so-called superstrings?

Paul: The superstring theory is just one of the latest in a series of attempts to unify all four forces, to amalgamate them into a single superforce. The essence of the superstring theory is that the world is made not out of particles, but string!

However, these unifying theories go beyond merely combining the forces. Quantum mechanics shows there is a very intimate link between the nature of particles and the nature of the forces. Let me explain. In everyday life we think of particles as lumps of matter, and forces as things that push and pull these lumps of matter; particles and forces are two quite separate kinds of physical thing. But at the level of atoms, and below, what you find is that the forces are best explained in terms of a traffic of particles – not particles of matter, but other sorts of particles.

Consider, for example, the electromagnetic force. If we have an electrical wire here, and a parallel electrical wire there, with currents passing through them, then there's a magnetic attraction between them. That is easy to demonstrate. We normally discuss this in terms of a magnetic field acting, or something. But at the atomic level the description changes. Instead, physicists like to think of electromagnetic forces as due to the exchange of particles called photons – they are related to light. And we think of these photons as rather like messengers; messengers that convey the force. Imagine that you have two electrons; we know that electric charges repel each other. We can understand this repulsive force at the atomic level as one electron sending out a messenger photon to the other electron saying, metaphorically, 'Hey, move!' And we can think of the operation of all four of the fundamental forces at the subatomic level as due to the exchange of these sorts of messenger particles.

Thus we have one list of particles over here – the particles of matter – which are being unified into families. There are lots and lots of them, but we feel that we can glimpse some sort of basic building blocks there. Then over there we have another lot of particles having to deal with the forces. Now, the great hope is that we can then bring about a further unification of the messenger particles and the matter particles into a single mathematical scheme, a single set of formulae. If so, it would merge together the description of the forces and the description of the particles of matter in one unifying supertheory. Wouldn't that be wonderful?

Phillip: You'll remember that marvellous image from antiquity that has the cosmos being carried on the back of a turtle. Others have postulated a whole succession of turtles beneath it. I've heard it said by people more scientifically literate than I am that, in a way, those turtles could represent tautologies – in the sense that every new theory is a magnificent, tautological restatement of things already known. In other words, theories explain theories which explain theories . . . or support theories.

Paul: No, I think that is wrong. I believe that what happens with scientific theories is when one theory replaces another it describes more – it's more powerful, more encompassing.

Phillip: A bigger turtle?

Paul: Yes. And the essence of the unification scheme I have been describing is that with each step in the amalgamation of things we reduce the total number of concepts, the total number of arbitrary features. We find linkages that were not previously known to exist, such as the connection between electricity and magnetism found by Faraday and Maxwell that reduced the number of basic forces that we need to describe the world. Einstein, too, found a link between entities that were previously considered distinct: between mass and energy, and between space and time. So new theories uncover further linkages between aspects of physics that were previously disparate.

Phillip: I like the way you talk and write about complexity – about the infinite complexity of this universe of ours. Yet here you are suggesting that there is another arrow, an arrow of simplification. At least a theoretical simplification of growing intellectual complexity.

Paul: Yes, that is right.

Phillip: Is that a paradox?

Paul: I don't think so. We started out with the Greek vision, which recognises that we live in a very complicated universe, and yet beneath it all there's a pleasing and harmonious simplicity. All the variety of different physical forms is simply due to the different atoms that they contain, arranged in different ways. This downward path from complicated big things to simple little things is fundamental to the whole program of physics – indeed all science – as it's been conducted over the last 300 years. Now it looks, as we approach the end of this millennium, that we might be on the verge of the final step, the culmination of this unification program: namely, getting to the bottom level of reality!

Phillip: Sorry, Paul. You know very well that that claim has been made many times in history.

Paul: Yes it has, but they were wrong in the past!

Phillip: Beware of hubris!

Paul: I think there is some reason for us to be fairly confident that we are now glimpsing, if not a final theory, at least the bottom level of reality. You know, we started out by talking about these atoms. Then I said that what we call atoms today are composite bodies, they have bits inside of them. Well, what have they got? There are electrons and then in the nuclei there are neutrons and protons. In the 1960s and 1970s it was deduced that even the neutrons and protons had bits inside of them: we give them the whimsical name of quarks.

You can conjecture there are bits inside the quarks, and so on; down and down we go like a set of Russian dolls. Maybe it's never-ending. However, I think that there is good evidence that with quarks, the various messenger particles that I have been talking about, electrons, neutrinos and a few other things, that this shopping list of particles is, as it were, almost the final list. We are nearing, or even at, the bottom level of reality. There isn't much further to go.

Actually, we would like to suppose that there is one more level left in this quest for the fundamental entities out of which the world is made. It would be nice if all the particles, whose names I've mentioned, are all made out of some single entity, some primitive thing, something which is truly indecomposable. It might not be a particle at all; it might be a little loop of string. This looks like the best current bet – an idea that seems sort of ludicrous, but is very fashionable at the moment – namely, the world isn't made out of tiny particles, tiny indestructible atoms, at all. The Greeks got it wrong. It is actually made out of little loops of string that wriggle around!

Phillip: There are many toiling in the vineyard of science, and many discoveries now seem to have a collective stamp on them, yet again and again the great breakthroughs seem to come from a single mind!

Paul: Yes!

Phillip: Is there such a mind lurking in a lab or standing in a lecture room somewhere at the moment?

Paul: It's often said that what we need is another Einstein to draw all these threads together. As you can tell from our discussion, we are stranded in a rather unsatisfactory and tentative state. We can glimpse certain unifications, but we lack that simple magic formula – simple enough for you to wear on your T-shirt – that would encapsulate at a stroke all of the particles and forces of nature in a single descriptive scheme. Perhaps what it needs is someone to come at this with a totally fresh approach, from a completely new angle, and weave it all together in a way that doesn't require huge expenditure on further experiments.

Phillip: But the name and address of this marvellous man or woman remains a mystery?

Paul: Well, from time to time various names and addresses are suggested. I won't mention them here, but speaking personally, I would say that there is nobody at the moment who seems to be coming at these problems with sufficient novelty and sufficient intellectual power to do for particle physics and the unification program what Einstein did for gravitation and space and time.

Phillip: There are many people who seem to believe that TOE equals G-O-D. But aren't you talking about a Theory of Everything that would *illuminate* scientific enquiry rather than close it down?

Paul: Absolutely right. You have to be very careful with the use of this TOE label – the theory of everything. What do we mean by 'everything' in this context? Suppose we had this magic formula that I could wear on my T-shirt, from which, by suitable mathematical manipulation, one could correctly describe all of the fundamental particles and forces of nature. Suppose we had at last identified the ultimate building blocks out of which the universe is put together. Supposing we had such a thing. Would it explain why people fall in love? Or why they vote in certain ways at elections? Or the movements of the stock market? No, of course not! It wouldn't even explain the origin of life, or the nature of consciousness.

In talking about a TOE, physicists refer to the culmination, not of physics, as such – the end would not be in sight of the whole of theoretical physics. What they are really talking about is the culmination of what we might call the reductionist program, begun in ancient Greece. Reductionism is the claim that we can explain the world by explaining the bits and pieces out of which the world is made. Thus, if only we can break open matter at a smaller and smaller scale and find the ultimate building blocks, then if we can understand these building blocks we will understand everything that exists.

I think this claim is total nonsense. To be sure, reductionism is a very important part of physical science. The reductionist program has been immensely successful in helping us to understand the universe. But it's only half the story.

Phillip: I'm glad you say that as a scientist. There are many in the anti-science push, and Brian Appleyard comes to mind, who would scream blasphemy at any claim that a theory of everything was about to be unveiled. Appleyard would brand that the ultimate example of reductionism. And reductionism is now the most lethal of pejoratives.

Paul: Reductionism has had a bad press. Partly this is because people confuse reductionism as a method, and reductionism as a total explanation of how things are, as a theory of everything. I had better just explain a bit more about reductionism. It is a way of describing the world by 'reducing' phenomena at a certain level of explanation, at a certain level of description, to processes at a smaller level – smaller in size, or at least simpler in explanation. It's often said that human beings can be reduced to biology, biology can be reduced to chemistry, and chemistry to physics. If you take a human being you reason thus: a person is nothing but a collection of cells, and cells are nothing but a collection of chemical reactions, and chemical reactions are nothing but a collection of atoms and molecules doing their thing. So ultimately human beings are nothing more than moving mounds of atoms.

Reductionism is an obnoxious philosophy because it seems to devalue so much that is important to us. Yet as a methodology it is extremely powerful. There is no doubt about it that physicists, breaking open matter and finding quarks and things inside, have made enormous advances in understanding the world. Also biologists, in breaking down cells into genes and understanding the genes, and the interaction between the proteins and DNA, and so on, have made enormous advances in unravelling the mysteries of life. But it's simply a mistake to assume that that has *got* to be the whole story.

Phillip: Or that it is a one-way street because, in a sense, fairly simple discoveries made it possible to build Gothic cathedrals. So you may be able, once you get this wonderful theory, to build on it in unimaginably complex ways!

Paul: That's true. We often talk as though there are two counter-directed arrows: the arrow of reductionism going down to the simplest building blocks, and then the arrow of holism which is going in the opposite direction, in the direction of the collective and organisational aspects of complex systems. But of course you can find linkages between the two. And for me, one of the most fascinating linkages is that the most complex system we know, namely the human brain which gives rise to consciousness, culture, mathematics, and so on, can find its most convincing application to the world down at that bottom level, to those mathematical symmetries that describe how matter is put together.

Phillip: Which may be, as you have said earlier, the universal language!

Paul: Mathematics is the language of nature, and yet it is also a product of the human mind. Isn't that absolutely fascinating? Isn't it incredible that something which comes out of this most complex system we know – the human brain – something that is a cultural construct, nevertheless finds its most powerful applications to the simplest and most basic components of the universe! That's what I find marvellous and inspiring, that 'looping back' of the complexity into the simplicity.

Phillip: I like it when you get excited. It's good to see you enthusiastic. Over dinner last night I was complaining of the fact that in this enormous universe, with its almost infinite number of available years, I've been allocated, if I'm lucky, a wretched 600 000-hour lifetime. Most of which, damn it, I've already expended. And wasted. You and I were discussing how many years we thought would constitute a reasonable deal, and we agreed we'd like a millennium. We wanted a thousand years each.

Paul: Yes, at least. I think we need a thousand years to solve a few problems!

Phillip: I'm happy for you to get your thousand provided you use it productively. Now, if we were to have this conversation in a thousand years' time there'd be a slight modification to the landscape around us.

Paul: Not much, I would suspect.

Phillip: Not a lot. But what about the mindscape? What would scientists be thinking about in a thousand years? Would the great intellectual journey be all but over? Would they simply be tinkering? Fine-tuning? Or would there still be extraordinary prospects for theorising?

Paul: It seems to me, looking back over my career, that we are living at a rather extraordinary time, when the pace of discovery, the pace of events, has been frenetic. It can't go on like that forever. But I come back to the fact that the reductionist program might be on the verge of completion. So in a thousand years we could open a textbook and there would be the magic formula! You could go down to your local supermarket and buy the T-shirt with the magic formula on the front.

However, it would be acknowledged that this formula fell short of being truly a theory of everything, so that when we move in the other direction, in the direction of ever-greater complexity, there are ever-more mysteries to solve. Phillip, there's a whole universe out there to explore! There may be any number of complicated physical forms, physical systems, that we could not explain with that simple theory of everything. So I'm sure there is going to be a lot left for us to do even in a thousand years.

Phillip: In that case it's badly named, isn't it, this TOE?

Paul: Yes, it's very badly named. It's not a theory of everything unless you're an out-and-out reductionist and believe that literally everything in the universe boils down to what individual subatomic particles, or little loops of string, or whatever it is, are going to do.

Phillip: I've always preferred questions to answers. Nonetheless I'd like to live long enough to see this particular T-shirt printed – to hear the theory expounded and to see how far it does go to explain the issues we've been discussing. Would a theory of *almost* everything help us much with the riddle of time?

Paul: Oh, yes!

Phillip: Would it help us much with consciousness?

Paul: No! Yes for time, no for consciousness! Because time is such a fundamental part of the physical universe. Time and space are interwoven and, as Einstein showed us, gravitation is a manifestation of the warping, or distortion, or curvature, of space-time. Any theory that amalgamates gravitation with the other forces of nature has to take care of space and time as well. So we would expect of this theory of everything, or not quite everything, not only a description of all the particles and forces of nature, but the answer to why there are apparently three dimensions of space (or maybe more with some of them hidden) and how this whole thing called the universe came into existence in the first place –

Phillip: And how it will end?

Paul: And how it will end! So it would be a theory of the fundamental matter and forces of nature, and of the origin and end of the universe; all in one marvellous formula, or set of formulae. At least, one textbook!

Phillip: Go on, Paul, show us the T-shirt. Come on, come on . . . the crew want to see the T-shirt!

Paul: Well, we've designed the T-shirt . . . it's the formulae we are having trouble with!

vi

What Does It All Mean?

Phillip: *Throughout our discussions here in the desert, Paul Davies and I have marvelled over the subtlety and beauty of nature. We've puzzled over the paradoxes of existence. We've celebrated the magic of the cosmos. But whereas we may agree on the scientific facts, we differ sharply on their interpretation. Paul has written several books on the metaphysical implications of science, but does the god that physicists talk about – and they often seem to – bear the slightest resemblance to the popular notions of a god I long ago rejected? And where does science stop and faith begin?*

Science versus faith, Paul, faith versus science. Is it not true that in a very profound sense science *is* a faith?

Paul: I think the whole of the scientific enterprise is founded on an act of faith. You can't be a scientist unless you believe that there is a really existing order in nature. Science is about uncovering that order. If you thought that the order in nature was merely some cultural construct – just something that we impose upon nature, something we read into nature rather than read out of nature – I don't think you could honestly be a scientist. You've got to believe that in following the scientific path, you're uncovering something that is really there.

Furthermore, you have to believe that this order which we see in nature is intelligible to us. After all, if we could make nothing of it then we would make no progress at all in science. So there is this huge act of faith that nature is both ordered and intelligible.

Phillip: Could the universe have been otherwise?

Paul: Einstein once said that the thing that most interested him was whether God had any choice in the nature of his creation (or perhaps we should say her creation). Although Einstein wasn't conventionally religious, he expressed using a theological metaphor a very real puzzle as to whether or not the order we see in nature is logically necessary. Might it be the case that if we knew enough about nature, if we had the theory of everything we were talking about, then we would find it to be the *only* logically consistent theory that there could be? In other words, that there is only one way in which the universe could be put together with logical and mathematical consistency? Under those circumstances, this would be the only possible universe, and there would be nothing left to explain (except, perhaps, why there exists any universe at all).

However, I do not believe this to be the case. It's the job of the theoretical physicist to invent imaginary model worlds: logically consistent universes that are not *this* universe, but some impoverished or simplified version thereof. Theoretical physicists often come up with simple mathematical models that would do as rather uninteresting universes. Well, we don't live in those. So it's very clear to me that the universe could have been otherwise, that the law-like order in nature of which I speak could have been different. And of course that begs the question, why this universe? Indeed, why any universe at all?

Phillip: I don't wish to sound scientifically blasphemous, but what is so special about this universe?

Paul: There are a number of special features when you look at it. The first thing concerns a topic we discussed earlier: that the laws of nature – the laws of physics – seem to be remarkably felicitous in the way they encourage matter and energy to become ever-more complex. These laws enable the universe to evolve from the featureless origins of the big bang to the richness and diversity we see today, including systems such as living organisms and thinking beings who can sit back and reflect on the meaning of it all. If you just picked any old rag-bag of laws, then the chances are you would either be led to a universe that was totally chaotic – cosmic anarchy – or something that would be so boring and repetitive that it wouldn't lead to anything very interesting at all. So that is one way in which the laws of physics are very special.

There are a number of other ways as well. Imagine playing the role of a deity, with a shopping list of laws in front of you, and you can pick from this long list of possible laws. Some laws are totally different from those in our universe – the real universe. Maybe there are also laws on the list that are very similar to, but not quite the same as, our own. Suppose you could twiddle a few knobs – to use a different analogy – and change a few features of the laws we know and love; that is, pick similar but slightly different laws from the list. I'm not talking here about moving physical objects around. I'm referring to such things as changing the strength of gravity, say, or the masses of some of the subatomic particles. A mathematical study very soon shows that if you were to change the present arrangement of things by very much, then the existence of complex structures, in particular of sentient beings, would almost certainly be impossible. In other words, unless the laws of physics had a form very similar to the actual laws, there would probably be no thinking beings in the universe to reflect on the matter. So it does seem there are a number of aspects in which the particular set of laws that apply to this actual universe are really rather special.

Phillip: Paul, let me raise an objection. Should intelligent beings be surprised if they find themselves in the universe which is appropriate and hospitable to intelligent beings?

Paul: Yes and no. It's no surprise that we exist here on the surface of a planet, for example, even though most of the universe is near-empty space. It is very obvious that life has evolved *here* because this is a suitable niche within the universe for life to flourish, even though it's a very atypical location. However, what I was talking about is not our spatial location or our temporal location, it is the underlying laws of the universe. And these laws are supposed to be universal and eternal; they apply everywhere, everywhen. What I'm saying is that the particular *laws* in this universe are very, very special.

Phillip: As an atheist, I put to you this: isn't it possible that other universes exist, or did exist, or will exist, where, because of slight variations on the theme, they don't play out as satisfactorily as ours, and is it not possible for conscious beings to sit around in them and rejoice in them?

Paul: Yes. It is often said that the world we live in is the world we *live* in. Imagine a vast assemblage of universes, each with slightly different laws, slightly different conditions. Perhaps in only a tiny fraction of those universes would circumstances be just right so that life and consciousness arise. And in those universes any sentient beings would perhaps rejoice in their good fortune. But they would be mistaken in supposing that there was any preordained design involved in their world, or their own existence, or that they had been selected in some way. In fact, they themselves would have selected the universe they live in, in the same way that Earth-life has selected the surface of a planet on which to arise, on account of its equable conditions, against the many vastly alternative, hostile, non-planetary locations that also exist.

The foregoing scenario is often presented as an antidote to any talk of design, and I think we have to take the argument seriously as a possibility. However I think there are some shortcomings in it. The most obvious shortcoming is that, by definition, these other worlds are not worlds we (or anyone else) are going to observe. They are independent of this universe. So we can't really falsify – we can't test – this hypothesis at all. It is not very scientific. Moreover, some people might think that invoking an infinity of unseen worlds just to explain the one we do see is even more extravagant than invoking an unseen god. So you have to be careful.

But I think there is a more serious objection, of a technical nature, which is this: the many-universes theory, in its strongest form, proposes that there are no laws – just chaos. In a very tiny fraction of the universes, law-like regularities appear purely by chance – as a result of statistical freaks, such as getting heads from a coin toss a million times in a row, or dealing a perfect suit at cards. Such events, which may be so unusual as to give the appearance of a rule, are in fact just accidents that are bound to occur somewhere if you have untold zillions of trials. But if the only thing that selects the ordered universes from the chaotic ones is the existence of life, then in a universe like ours (that contains life) you would only expect to see a level of order to a degree that is just necessary for life to be maintained. Any additional order, over and above this minimal level required for life, would be exceedingly improbable, for the same reason that tossing a billion heads in a row is exceedingly less likely than merely tossing a million heads. However, there are many law-like aspects of our universe which are such that, if those laws were to fail or falter just a bit, would *not* constitute a threat to life.

Phillip: For instance?

Paul: Well, let me give you an example. If the law of conservation of electric charge, which is a very fundamental law of physics, should falter – if it should get a little bit wobbly, so to speak – then what would be the consequences for life of small fluctuations in the magnitude of atomic charges? Well, as far as chemistry and biology are concerned, absolutely nothing. There would be no way in which small variations of electric charge would be life-threatening. We could still exist happily in such a universe. We could still be having this conversation. And so if you are going to argue that the existence of life is somehow selecting, from what is ultimately just chaos, the *appearance* of law, you would expect to see chaos in all those aspects of nature that are not relevant for biological survival – including random deviations from order on a scale that is too small to have any biological consequences, and yet is still observable. If nature's order is just selected from chaos, then every time you see law-like aspects in nature, *any* sort of contravention or faltering of those apparent laws should threaten the existence of life – and it clearly doesn't. In other words the law-like order in nature is just too good, it's too refined, to be explained simply as selection effect – that we only see a lawful universe because that is the only universe we could live in.

Phillip: How does your view differ from the anthropic view?

Paul: I suppose I should just explain the so-called anthropic principle, which was introduced into science by Brandon Carter about twenty years ago. It comes in a weak and a strong version. In the weak version it simply says that sentient living organisms (like humans) will exist only in a universe, or a part of a universe, that is consistent with biology; that is, consistent with the emergence of complexity and consciousness. That's just really a tautology. No one would object to that; it's obviously true. I already gave a trivial example of the weak anthropic principle concerning life existing on the surface of the Earth. We don't exist out there in empty space

There is, however, a stronger version of the anthropic principle, which I think a lot of people would object to, which says there is some element of compulsion: that the universe *must* be such as to arrange its laws and conditions in order that life and consciousness should emerge to observe it. In other words, it takes the point of view that a universe that goes unobserved is a meaningless concept.

Phillip: A universe not worth having, in a way!

Paul: Sort of. So this strong anthropic principle somehow implies there is a rather deep link between the existence of conscious beings and the laws that give rise to them. Now, I think many scientists would be happy – all scientists would probably be happy – with the weak version of the anthropic principle. Very few would be happy with the strong version.

However, this discussion about the fact that you can't have any old universe and still have conscious beings, or at least certainly not conscious beings of the sort we are familiar with, is a very useful one because it shows that in some sense the laws of physics are rather special. Now, some people just dismiss that fact and say, 'So what? If it hadn't been that way we wouldn't be here to worry about it!' Well, you can take that attitude. You can shrug your shoulders and say, 'Well, we are jolly lucky that that is how the universe is.' You accept the rather remarkably special lawfulness of the universe as a brute fact, as just 'given' – reasonlessly. But to me it does suggest something a little bit deeper.

Phillip: But it seems to me your argument is taking us to a position where once again we – life – our life – seems to be crucial to this progress!

Paul: It depends on what you mean by 'we' here. I think you are raising a very important point. The anthropic principle sounds very much like *homo sapiens* back at the centre of the universe, and that is definitely not what is intended (in spite of the somewhat unfortunate term 'anthropic'). Most of the investigations that try to determine the conditions out of which life will emerge simply draw a very broad picture and just talk about, say, carbon-based life (the existence of carbon being crucial to Earth-life). There is no suggestion that life on Earth, still less our own species, is a key part in this. The anthropic argument simply says that if somewhere and somewhen, in the unfolding drama of the universe, some sort of sentient beings are going to emerge, then this places rather stringent conditions on the nature of the laws of physics. And the fact that the real universe *has* those conditions is very suggestive, but that's all. It is merely circumstantial evidence for something deeper, something, as I like to say, 'going on'. But you don't have to draw that conclusion. You could just say, 'Well, it is just jolly lucky that it is so, and I won't enquire deeper'. However, if you are interested in the underlying issues – the deeper metaphysical issues – in the 'why' behind the 'how' – you are inevitably struck by what seems to be some extraordinary coincidences in the laws of nature.

Phillip: You have mentioned design, which of course suggests a designer, but before we look at that, is it not true that Darwin disposed of the notion of design?

Paul: The design argument for the existence of God, the so-called watchmaker argument, was very popular a couple of hundred years ago, largely from a study of biological systems. The essence of the argument is that, just as you can tell from inspection of its innards that a watch had been designed by an intelligence for a purpose, so too can you see from the clever arrangement of the parts of a living organism that it has been designed for a purpose. Well, you are absolutely right that this argument was demolished by Darwin's theory of evolution, because there is a very good mechanism – namely, variation and natural selection – that can produce the *appearance* of design even when there is no design. So if you ask me about features such as the human eye, which seems so well adapted to its purpose, I wouldn't have said that, as a specific entity, the eye is an example of design. We can understand how, if you have an ensemble of competing organisms, and competing species, then that competition can lead to the emergence of very clever-looking organs.

I accept that Darwinian picture. But the appearance of design I'm talking about refers not to the objects of the universe – not to the specific physical systems – but to the underlying laws. And the difficulty you have if you want to argue along Darwinian lines is that, somehow, the laws have emerged as a result of natural selection. But we don't readily see anything like a population of universes with a population of competing laws slugging it out, you know, red in tooth and claw, so that only a universe that is felicitously adapted, as far as the emergence of life is concerned, comes out at the end as the survivor. I might say that there have been some rather crude attempts by some physicists and cosmologists to link a sort of cosmic Darwinism to Darwinism on Earth, but I don't find these attempts very convincing.

So I think that when we are dealing with the universe, and the laws of the universe (and for all we know there is only one universe and one set of laws), it's very hard to use this sort of Darwinian mechanism to explain the appearance of design.

Phillip: So we are not looking for a watchmaker but we are looking for a legislator?

Paul: Precisely!

Phillip: Using such arguments as led to you being accused of the sin, of the heresy, of teleology. Perhaps you should explain the term.

Paul: Teleology is the belief in final causes. It's a very ancient idea, going back to Aristotle at least. Briefly, it is the notion that a physical system, maybe the whole universe, is being drawn towards some preordained final state – perhaps there is some sort of guiding hand of the divine that somehow manipulates or encourages physical systems towards this final destiny – which is somehow written down in advance. This type of teleology is anathema to scientists. I might say that it's anathema to me as well, in the version that there is a final cosmic destiny already decided.

I've tried to introduce a notion that I

whimsically call 'teleology without teleology'. Imagine that the laws of physics – the laws of nature in general – are specially chosen to have the following clever property. They don't fix the final state in detail, but they encourage or facilitate a general trend; namely, the evolution of matter and energy along certain pathways towards greater organisational complexity. So the outcome of these processes is assuredly interesting, but it is not determined in detail.

There's a very simple analogy that I like to use concerning the game of chess. If I give you a checkerboard and some pieces, and ask you to invent a game, the chances are that if you pick any old set of rules then the game would be either very repetitive and boring or almost certainly just totally chaotic. Either way the game would be uninteresting. Now, the actual rules of chess have of course have been very, very carefully selected to lead to a rich and interesting variety of play. But having decided the rules of chess, the specific details of any given game are not fixed in advance – that depends on the play. And so here we see this exquisite mix of chance and necessity that I have been referring to throughout these discussions. The laws of physics are like the rules of chess and the game is like the working out of the universe, the great cosmic experiment. And the end isn't fixed – it's open. However, these clever laws encourage or facilitate certain types of evolutionary behaviour that look very interesting – that lead to complexity and organisation, for example, that mimic the effect of teleology, that make it seem *as if* many physical systems have been designed in advance for a final cause. The individual systems have *not* been thus designed, but there is still a hint of design in the underlying laws themselves.

I might say that it is *far* more ingenious to produce a universe of the sort we observe from the outworking of fixed and inviolable laws than it is to assemble it piecemeal by tinkering, after the fashion of the designer God of old.

Phillip: As an atheist, I'm constantly pointing out to devotees of this or that faith that most religions have a use-by date. Odin, Thor, Vulcan, Zeus, Ra – they're all gone. The pantheon is emptying. And I've always argued that as science advances, God – the god-of-the-gaps – recedes. But the god-of-the-gaps is one of the many gods you don't like.

Paul: Absolutely. I've never liked the notion of a cosmic magician – a sort of superbeing who lives in the sky, or beyond the sky, who created everything in the first place, and who intervenes from time to time to fix up the world when things go wrong. This is the god-of-the-gaps you referred to. The term arises from the notion that at any given time we understand only part of the natural world around us, so there are gaps in our knowledge, and therefore that is the place to insert a god. So when lightning and thunder were a mystery, why, the god Thor produced them! But of course, as science advances so those gaps get smaller and smaller, and God – or the gods – are squeezed out of them until he or she or they are squeezed off the edge of space and time altogether, and appear to be totally redundant. You're on a hiding to nothing, I think, if you want to invoke some sort of supernatural superbeing – a cosmic magician – to intervene from time to time to work miracles.

As a scientist, I find the notion of miracles utterly repugnant, first of all because I rejoice in the lawfulness of the universe and in the beautiful nature of the laws of physics, and I hate to think of them being arbitrarily broken. But secondly, I wouldn't think too much of a being who creates a flawed universe, and then meddles with it fitfully.

Phillip: Tinkered with, fine-tuned?

Paul: The idea of a universe which has laws that are so clever – where things work so well that the universe can take care of itself – where the laws of nature can perform the necessary miracles – is much more inspiring. So I say there are no miracles other than the miracle of nature itself!

Phillip: Your work is frequently appropriated by New Agers or, in my view, misrepresented by some Christian theologians. So it's important for you to be clear about your beliefs and disbeliefs. I know you don't believe in a personal god.

Paul: There are really two sorts of gods that have been around for some time. We might crudely say that one of these – the personal god – is the god concerned with human behaviour, morality, preservation of life after death. This is a guardian-angel type of god. I would love to believe there is such a being, but I find it very difficult to do so. Then we've got the other sort of god; much more remote, much more powerful – in a sense much more awesome. This is God the great architect of the cosmos, an abstract, timeless being that is somehow responsible for the overall organisation and structure and lawfulness of the universe.

Most of the world's religions try to merge these two characteristics – God the creator of the grand scheme, and the personal god. And they have a lot of difficulty! Christianity had to adopt a Trinity – to have three gods – before it could really sort out all the required qualities. Whilst I'd love to believe in a guardian-angel, personal god, I find it very difficult as a scientist to do so. However, when it comes to this – and I hesitate to even use the word god – this felicitous, pleasing, harmonious, almost contrived, and especially *ingenious* nature of the lawfulness of the cosmos (it is the ingenuity that I find most inspiring), then, to me, that cries out for something like 'meaning' or 'purpose'. I realise both of those words are loaded, and we have to use them very carefully, but something like meaning or purpose, or at least rationality, surely lies behind it all.

One important point I think we have to confront here: discussions of this sort often get hung up on an old argument, sometimes called the cosmological argument for the existence of God, that runs into a major problem. If you are using God to explain the universe you get into the problem of who created God.

Phillip: Exactly the question I was going to put to you. As a child I could not accept the notion of God. Adults would insist that you needed a god to begin things. I'd immediately counter with, 'Who began God?' And I'd go off and get a clip over the ears for being cheeky. Yet it seems to me an immensely powerful question.

Paul: And a very legitimate question. People often ask what made the big bang go bang. Who created the universe? There must have been something there, they say, before the big bang. Somebody or something must have started it all off! Perhaps God the great architect, the creator god.

Well, I was at pains to point out earlier that modern physics, and indeed one strand of the Christian tradition going back to Augustine, insists that time itself came into existence *with* the big bang; the universe began with time and not in time. That point is absolutely fundamental. We are not talking about some super-being or force or power that was there before the universe, 'before' in the temporal sense. I reject the notion of a being who floats there for all eternity, then presses a button, so that – bang! – the universe appears, and then sits back to watch the action, or maybe interferes with it from time to time. So I am not talking about something that was there before. I am talking about something which is timeless – something outside of time, indeed space, altogether.

The closest analogy that I can get to the sort of timeless, abstract being – maybe it's more than just an analogy – is mathematics. If you ask the question, 'Where is the number eleven?' well, it isn't anywhere. It's not in space, it's not in time. Or consider the statement: eleven is a prime number. This is a true statement whether there is a universe here or not. Mathematical objects and statements reside in an abstract, timeless realm that transcends the physical universe, yet they apply to the physical universe, too.

Phillip: What you are proposing is not going to hold your hand on your deathbed, though. This proposition is not going to calm you when you look at mortality. It is too remote and chilling a notion, isn't it?

Paul: It is. Many people have no time for this abstract, great-architect notion of God; they are only interested in the guardian angel, and I can understand that.

Phillip: But Paul, there are many who will accept *any* definition of a god that a scientist provides, no matter how austere or chilling a god that might be. They'll rush to you and say, 'Thanks very much.'

Paul: Yes, that is the problem with the word. I don't like using the word god at all, although what I am describing, I have to say, comes rather close to the conception of god that many modern Christian theologians have. I don't find there's a great deal of difference when I talk to them.

Phillip: You're talking about the more sophisticated and progressive theologians.

Paul: Absolutely right. But it is a world away from the concept of god that comes across from the pulpit on a Sunday.

Phillip: Do you remember we were talking previously about how the term big bang was recently reviewed by scientists in the hope they could find a better term? Perhaps it's time for you to apply your considerable intellect to finding a better word than god!

Paul: We want a word that in some way captures the ingenuity and rationality of nature. For me, science is an intellectual exercise, and if you are solving a puzzle, you can't help but feel somebody – or something – set the puzzle in the first place. Then this word should include something of the cryptic or hidden aspect, because the laws of nature which I have been talking about, and celebrating, are not obvious to us at a glance. We do not look around and see Newton's laws of motion, for example. If we see the apple fall, we see a falling apple. We do not see a set of differential equations.

Phillip: Well, I see a falling apple. I'm sure you do see a set of differential equations.

Paul: I see exactly the same as you. To get at the underlying laws we have to be really rather clever. We have to go through all sorts of arcane procedures – using mathematical analysis, laboratory experiments, and so on. You have to work rather hard to dig out these underlying laws of nature.

Take the field that we were talking about in an earlier discussion, fundamental particle physics, and the abstract symmetries there. You have to work very hard indeed to dig out those laws. So it is almost as if the laws of nature are written in code and that doing science amounts to breaking the code.

Phillip: And you need a special priesthood to do the code-breaking, too!

Paul: After a fashion, yes. Well, it is an extraordinary thing that humans have this decoding ability, that nature is intelligible to us, that we are able to crack the cosmic code. But to believe this cosmic code is somehow self-generating, self-flying, self-sustaining, strains credulity. It seems to me that somehow our ability to break the code, and the existence of the code, have to be linked in a deep way. But not in the crass way of 'in the beginning there was some sort of being who we don't explain, and the being invented a code, and a universe, and plonked humans in it'. I won't have that! It is something much more subtle – and much more inspiring, and because we are removing time from the picture, it is not a matter of a *causal* sequence of events here. I have in mind something which is more of a logical interweaving of different conceptual levels.

So we are beginning to tease out a much more sophisticated notion of meaning or purpose here – not a linear chain of causation or explanation, but more of a holistic interconnectedness (logical, not physical interconnectedness). Science deals with the physical world, but supposes that this physical world is underpinned by an abstract logical and mathematical world, wherein resides the rational basis of existence. It is the latter domain that the theoretical physicist explores, and it is there, in my view, that we find the most fruitful interplay of scientific and theological concepts. So when I use the word god, which I do reluctantly, I mean something like 'that which underpins or guarantees this mathematical law-like order in nature'. It's the thing that interweaves and underpins and guarantees it all.

Phillip: Shortly before he died, I interviewed that considerable Australian historian Professor Manning Clark, and Manning confessed to me that he had a 'shy belief' in the existence of

God. Now it seems to me that you have more than a shy belief but less than a certainty. Am I right?

Paul: It is certainly less than a certainty . . .

List of Players

Bryan Appleyard (1951–)
>British journalist, commentator and author of *Understanding the Present* (1992), an attack on scientific hubris.

Aristotle (384–322 BC)
>Greek philosopher, pupil of Plato, tutor of Alexander the Great, influenced Islamic philosophers and Christian theologians.

Saint Augustine of Hippo (354–430 BC)
>Fifth-century theologian, influential in the early Christian church. Author of *The City of God* and *Confessions*. Noted for his ideas on creation and the nature of time.

Brandon Carter (1942–)
>British theoretical astrophysicist, now working in France, and originator of the so-called anthropic principle. Noted for his work on black holes.

Professor Manning Clark (1914–91)
> Notable Australian historian. In 1975 he received the Companion of the Order of Australia in recognition of his major work, *A History of Australia*.

Charles Darwin (1809–82)
> British naturalist, author of *On the Origin of Species* (1859) and originator of the theory of evolution by natural selection.

René Descartes (1596–1650)
> French philosopher and mathematician who introduced the philosophical theory of dualism; a split between mind and body.

Freeman Dyson (1923–)
> British-born theoretical physicist who has worked mainly at the Institute for Advanced Study in Princeton, USA. His books include *Disturbing the Universe* (1980) and *Infinite in all Directions* (1988). Noted for his bold and free-ranging ideas on space travel, technology and the future.

Sir Arthur Stanley Eddington (1882–1944)
> British astronomer, physicist and author. He was influential in popularising science in the pre-war years. Noted for his work on stars, and his offbeat ideas about relativity and cosmology.

Albert Einstein (1879–1955)
> German-born theoretical physicist who formulated

the theory of relativity (1905 and 1915) and laid the foundations for much of the twentieth-century physics. Awarded the Nobel Prize in 1922.

Michael Faraday (1791–1867)

British physicist and chemist; discovered the laws of electromagnetic induction and established the principles of electrolysis.

Alexander Friedman (1888–1925)

Russian meteorologist and physicist who is credited with being the first to use Einstein's theory of relativity to produce the standard mathematical models that describe an expanding universe.

Galileo Galilei (1564-1642)

Italian physicist, astronomer and mathematician, who built the first astronomical telescope (1609) and made observations supporting the Copernican model of the solar system. He was persecuted by the Church for his scientific ideas.

George Gamow (1904–68)

Russian-born physicist and cosmologist who worked mainly in the United States. Credited with formulating a detailed version of the big bang theory of the origin of the universe in the 1940s and 1950s. He predicted the existence of a hot early cosmic phase, and the survival of a cosmic background of heat radiation from the big bang.

Murray Gell-Mann (1929–)

US theoretical physicist, awarded the Nobel Prize in 1969. One of the originators of the quark theory of nuclear matter. In 1984 he helped establish the interdisciplinary Santa Fe Institute for the study of complexity.

Thomas Gold (1920–)

Astronomer and cosmologist, noted for proposing the steady state theory of the universe (with Hermann Bondi and Fred Hoyle) and for explaining the nature of pulsars.

Stephen Hawking (1942–)

British mathematician and physicist, noted for his work on black holes and cosmology. Author of the best selling popular science book *A Brief History of Time* (1988).

Hermann von Helmholtz (1821–94)

German physicist. Famous for his contributions to electromagnetism and thermodynamics.

Sir Fred Hoyle (1915–)

British theoretical astronomer and writer, associated with the steady state theory of the universe, arch opponent of the big bang theory. Noted for his bold and challenging theories on a range of scientific topics.

Edwin Powell Hubble (1889–1953)

US astronomer and pioneer in extragalactic astronomy who discovered that the universe is expanding.

Sir James Hopwood Jeans (1877–1946)

British mathematician, physicist and astronomer; best known for his work in statistical mechanics and his theory of the origin of the solar system. A great populariser of science and its philosophical ramifications.

Arthur Koestler (1905–83)

British novelist and essayist born in Budapest, Hungary. From 1956 he became immersed in questions of science and mysticism, and had a huge following among young people.

James Clerk Maxwell (1831–79)

British physicist who made major contributions to the theory of thermodynamics and electromagnetism. He predicted the existence of radio waves.

Jacques Monod (1910–76)

French biologist, Director of the Institut Pasteur in Paris. He won the Nobel Prize for Medicine and Physiology in 1965. His pioneering popular book *Chance and Necessity* (1972) introduced modern molecular biology and the theory of evolution to a wide public.

Sir Isaac Newton (1642–1727)

> English scientist, mathematician and philosopher; formulator of the laws of motion and gravitation, co-inventor of the calculus. He is credited with being one of the founders of modern science.

Roger Penrose (1931–)

> British mathematician and physicist, famous for his work on gravitation and cosmology, especially the theory of black holes and space-time singularities. He has speculated on the nature of the mind and brain.

Plato (427?–347 BC)

> Greek philosopher who enormously influenced the thought, religion and art of the Western world.

Ilya Prigogine (1917–)

> Belgian chemist and Nobel Prize winner of 1977. Famous for his work on non-equilibrium thermodynamics and dissipative systems.

Bertrand Russell (1872–1970)

> British philosopher, mathematician, pacifist, atheist and prolific writer, who won the Nobel Prize for Literature in 1950. Famous for his formulation of the logical foundations of mathematics.

Oliver Sacks (1933–)

> British-born physician and author, currently Professor of Neurology at Albert Einstein College in New York. Author and populariser of cognitive science.

Carl Edward Sagan (1934–)

US planetary scientist and writer. He played a leading role in the Mariner, Viking and Voyager expeditions to the planets. Pulitzer Prize winner, 1978.

Abdus Salam (1926–)

Pakistani-born theoretical physicist who has worked mainly in Britain and Italy. Former Director of the International Centre for Theoretical Physics in Trieste. Famous for his theory (with Steven Weinberg and Sheldon Glashow) of the unification of the electromagnetic and weak nuclear forces, for which he won the 1979 Nobel Prize in Physics.

Steven Weinberg (1933–)

US theoretical physicist and cosmologist, noted for his work on the unification of the fundamental forces of nature and the physics of the early universe. Shared the Nobel Prize in 1979 with Abdus Salam and Sheldon Glashow. Author of the popular books *The First Three Minutes* (1983) and *Dreams of a Final Theory* (1992).

Hermann Weyl (1885–1955)

German mathematician and physicist, noted for his work on group theory, field theory and relativity.

John Wheeler (1943–)

US theoretical physicist. Worked with Niels Bohr on nuclear theory, established the foundations of much of modern gravitational theory, and coined the term 'black hole'.